T0194583

In The Pursuit of Holiness

"Growing from Milk to Meat!"
—
Revised Edition

CALVIN L. MCCULLOUGH SR.

WESTBOW
PRESS®
A DIVISION OF THOMAS NELSON
& ZONDERVAN

WestBow Press books may be ordered through booksellers or by contacting:

WestBow Press
A Division of Thomas Nelson & Zondervan
1663 Liberty Drive
Bloomington, IN 47403
www.westbowpress.com
844-714-3454

ISBN: 978-1-6642-4596-9 (sc)
ISBN: 978-1-6642-4597-6 (hc)
ISBN: 978-1-6642-4595-2 (e)

Library of Congress Control Number: 2021919810

Print information available on the last page.

WestBow Press rev. date: 10/13/2021

Contents

Foreword... ix

Dedication xi

Introduction... xiii

Chapter 1   "Understanding Our Sanctification" 1

Chapter 2   "What does Jesus want most from me?" 14

Chapter 3   "Totally Surrendering All" 28

Chapter 4   "Separation from this World" 40

Chapter 5   "Understanding Who I Really Am" 55

Chapter 6   "Christian Community"............................... 71

Chapter 7   "The Christian Response to the World"................ 83

Chapter 8   "The Christian View of SEX"......................... 101

Chapter 9   "Worship and Praise"............................... 127

Chapter 10   "The Importance of the Church" 151

The Conclusion.. 171

References 173

Foreword

Father God, I know that I have broken Your laws and my sins have separated me from You.

I am truly sorry. And now I want to turn away from my past sinful life and turn towards you.

Please forgive me and help me avoid sinning again. I believe that Your son Jesus Christ died for my sins; He was resurrected from the dead; I believe He is alive and hears my prayer.

I invite You, Jesus, to become the Lord of my life; to rule and reign in my heart from this day forward.

Now, please send Your Holy Spirit to help me to obey You and to do Your will for the rest of my life. In Jesus' name I pray, Amen."

So now I've said the "Sinners Prayer;" I've asked the Lord Jesus Christ into my heart, and I know that I am a born-again child of God. Is that all it takes? Most Christians would probably say yes. But now it begs the question: How am I supposed to live my life until God calls me home?

The answer is that in our lives, we are to pursue the quality of holiness of Jesus and the Father, the progressive part of our sanctification.

This book is a tool we can use to redirect our lives and the lives of others as we fulfill the call and the command that every Christian has on their life . . . and it is to live holy and pleasing lives unto God the Father. The Bible tells us: "For God did not call us to be impure, but to live a holy life" (1 Thessalonians 4:7 NIV).

This book will demonstrate just how Jesus and the Apostles lived in this fallen and sinful world as examples of holiness while giving us instructions about holy living.

The writer of Hebrews gives us clear direction, "Let us fix our eyes on Jesus, the author and perfecter of our faith, who for the joy set before him endured the cross, scorning its shame, and sat down at the right hand of the throne of God" (Hebrews 12:2 BSB).

The Apostle Paul would say to us, "Follow my example, as I follow the example of Christ" (1 Corinthians 11:1 NIV).

Let us begin our journey "In the Pursuit of Holiness!"

Dedication

"This Book is dedicated to our Lord Jesus Christ, the true teacher and the perfecter of our Holiness!" Jesus, we thank You for your love, your mercy, your peace, and your grace. We thank You, Jesus, for the blood You shed so we may share in Your righteousness and gain a right relationship with God the Father through You.

In Loving Memory of my Mother
Arleaner McCullough Ingram

Introduction

As a Christian and disciple of Jesus Christ we are all called to be holy in all we do and say. If we looked through the Bible, we would find there are over a hundred verses in the Old and New Testament commanding holiness.

- Leviticus 11:44-45 (NIV), "I am the Lord your God; consecrate yourselves and be holy, because I am holy. Do not make yourselves unclean by any creature that moves along the ground. I am the Lord, who brought you up out of Egypt to be your God; therefore, be holy, because I am holy."

- Leviticus 19:2 (NKJV), "'Speak to all the congregation of the children of Israel, and say to them: 'You shall be holy, for I the LORD your God am holy.'"

- Leviticus 20:7 (NKJV), "Consecrate yourselves therefore, and be holy, for I am the LORD your God."

- Leviticus 20:26 (NIV), "You are to be holy to me because I, the LORD, am holy, and I have set you apart from the nations to be my own."

- 1 Corinthians 1:2 (BSB), "To the church of God in Corinth, to those sanctified in Christ Jesus and called to be holy, together with all those everywhere who call on the name of our Lord Jesus Christ, their Lord and ours."

- Ephesians 1:4 (NIV), "For he chose us in him before the creation of the world to be holy and blameless in his sight. In love."

- 1 Thessalonians 4:7 (NIV): "For God did not call us to be impure, but to live a holy life."

- Hebrews 12:14 (NIV), "Make every effort to live in peace with everyone and to be holy; without holiness no one will see the Lord."

- 1 Peter 1:15-16 (NKJV), "but as He who called you is holy, you also be holy in all your conduct, because it is written, "Be holy, for I am holy."

- Revelation 22:11 (ESV), "Let the evildoer still do evil, and the filthy still be filthy, and the righteous still do right, and the holy still be holy."

- And the list goes on!

God has commanded us to Be holy, because He is Holy. So, what is Holy or Holiness?

So, what does the word "Holy" mean?

I have found that there are four key elements in the meaning of Holiness:

- First, Holy or Holiness is God's distinguishing characteristic that separates Him from all His creation; 1 Samuel 2:2 (BSB) states, "There is no one holy like the LORD. Indeed, there is no one besides You! And there is no Rock like our God."

- Second, holiness is a distinct ethical purity; Leviticus 19:2 (NIV) says, "Speak to the entire assembly of Israel and say to them: 'Be holy because I, the LORD your God, am holy.'"

- Third, holiness is the moral idea for Christians as they seek to reflect the character of God as known in Jesus Christ; 1 Peter 1:15-16 (BSB) states, "But just as He who called you is holy, so be holy in all you do, for it is written: "Be holy, because I am holy.""

- And the fourth meaning of holiness is having a spiritually pure quality; Paul tells us, "And this I pray, that your love may abound yet more and more in knowledge and all discernment, for you to approve the things being excellent, so that you may be pure and blameless unto the day of Christ, being filled with the fruit of righteousness that is through Jesus Christ, to the glory and praise of God" (Philippians 1:9-11 BLB).

First, understand that Jesus Christ set the standard for holiness in the book of Matthew Chapter Five. We know it as the Sermon on the Mount. In His teaching, Jesus tells us, "Be perfect, therefore, as your heavenly Father is perfect." This is the highest standard for man. It is very important that we understand the foundation that Jesus has set in the book of

Matthew, so that we may obtain all that He has taken hold for us. In this way we may live our lives in a pleasing manner before our Father.

Here, Jesus instructs us about holiness, and he also models it for us. Additionally, we find that the Apostles give us instructions about holiness, and they too, model it. In doing so, we show that through the Blood of Jesus Christ and the power of the Holy Spirit, we can obtain holiness. So, let's look at this Sermon on the Mount as we begin our pursuit of holiness.

One of the first things we find is that the Lord Jesus identifies the type of person that is truly a blessed person in the eyes of the Father. We must understand that He is looking at the attitude or heart of the people that He's called blessed. This Christian attitude is exemplified in the Beatitudes. The Be-attitudes should be the attitudes of all true Christians. The author, Matthew, beautifully illustrates what the heartbeat of every true Christian in this dark world should be and what's at the heart of God/Jesus!

The Beatitudes are not called the Do-attitudes; meant to convey they are a list of things we should do. That would make the Christian life a life of works and rules, in-which it is not. It's important to note that the Be-attitudes describe Godly character and attitude that come only through the power of the Holy Spirit and faith in the Lord Jesus Christ.

In the book of Matthew, Jesus points out that the true followers pursue righteousness and purity even amidst insults and persecution.

> "Blessed are the poor in spirit, for theirs is the kingdom of heaven. Blessed are those who mourn, for they will be comforted. Blessed are the meek, for they will inherit the earth. Blessed are those who hunger and thirst for righteousness, for they will be filled. Blessed are the merciful, for they will be shown mercy. Blessed are the pure in heart, for they will see God. Blessed are the peacemakers, for they will be called children of God. Blessed are those who are persecuted because of righteousness, for theirs is the kingdom of heaven. "Blessed are you when people insult you, persecute you and falsely say all kinds of evil against you because of

me. Rejoice and be glad, because great is your reward in heaven, for in the same way they persecuted the prophets who were before you" (Matthew 5:3-12 NIV).

Second, Jesus, the true light of the world, points out "Who" and "What" we are. He calls believers Salt and Light to express and show the impact Christians make in this world, thereby bringing glory, honor, and praise to God the Father.

"You are the salt of the earth. But if the salt loses its saltiness, how can it be made salty again? It is no longer good for anything, except to be thrown out and trampled underfoot. "You are the light of the world. A town built on a hill cannot be hidden. Neither do people light a lamp and put it under a bowl. Instead, they put it on its stand, and it gives light to everyone in the house. In the same way, let your light shine before others, that they may see your good deeds and glorify your Father in heaven" (Matthew 5:13-16 NIV).

Next Jesus tells everyone what His role and mission was. He came to fulfill prophecy in scriptures and God's moral law. God's ceremonial and moral law was given in order to help mankind love God with our total being: mind, body, and soul. Jesus came to give and help us understand a deeper meaning, which moves from the outward act of religion into an internal act of love that flows from the heart of God the Father.

Further in Matthew, Jesus' message is continued. In it, He points out to us that the religious leaders and teachers of that day had only an outward religion.

"Do not think that I have come to abolish the Law or the Prophets; I have not come to abolish them but to fulfill them. For truly I tell you, until heaven and earth disappear, not the smallest letter, not the least stroke of a pen, will by any means disappear from the Law until everything is accomplished. Therefore, anyone who sets aside one of the least of these commands and teaches others accordingly will be called least in the kingdom of heaven, but whoever practices and teaches these commands will be called great in the kingdom of heaven. For I tell you that unless your righteousness surpasses that of the Pharisees and the teachers of the law, you will certainly not enter the kingdom of heaven" (Matthew 5:17-20 NIV).

In the second part of verse nineteen, we find a key to the Pursuit of Holiness; it says, "whoever practices and teaches these commands will be called great in the kingdom of heaven."

We find that most Christians say that they love Jesus with their mouths, but their hearts and their actions don't line up with what they say. Here Jesus tells us that if we want to be called great in heaven, we must practice and teach His commands.

In the next section of Jesus' message, he talks about our relationship with others and how Christians are to respond to others in a fallen, sinful world. He has laid the foundation of His message in the opening statement of Beatitudes. He now proceeds with five examples (murder, sexual sins, making oaths, and responding to your enemies) in order to show the true spirit of the law lived out through the hearts of true followers and disciples.

Note: The areas in which Jesus is spoke of is, murder, sexual sins, making oaths, and responding to your enemies; will be explained in further detail in Chapter Six through Chapter Eight.

Please understand that the purpose of this book is to help new and not so new Christians understand how to live out their progressive (or the pursuing) part of their sanctification. So, let's start by getting a better understanding of what sanctification is in Chapter One.

Chapter One

"Understanding Our Sanctification"

"It's what Jesus did for us!"

In order to have a clear biblical understanding of our sanctification, we should take a look at regeneration, justification and glorification and how they all work together in the lives of Christians. Understand what these terms mean, and the distinctions between them will clearly show us that salvation is past, present and future - spirit, soul, and body.

It is truly important that we understand that all the benefits of our salvation are connected to us through our relationship with Jesus Christ. It is by Jesus, through Jesus, and because of Jesus we have received regeneration, justification, sanctification and glorification, because outside of a relationship with Him there is no salvation.

Regeneration

First let's start with regeneration; this word in the Greek language is *gennao* which means new birth, rebirth, or reproduction. Regeneration is God's work in the believer at conversion to create a new person empowered by the Holy Spirit.[1] This means that at your conversion you were made into a new creation in Christ Jesus and your spirit was regenerated and renewed from your old spirit and behavior into a new spirit and behavior.

- "He saved us, not because of the righteous things we had done, but because of his mercy. He washed away our sins, giving us a new birth and new life through the Holy Spirit" (Titus 3:5 NLT).

- "Therefore, if anyone is in Christ, he is a new creation; old things have passed away; behold, all things have become new" (2 Corinthians 5:17 KJV).

- "Jesus replied, "I tell you the truth, unless you are born again, you cannot see the Kingdom of God" (John 3:3 NLT).

The new birth is the most extreme change in a person's life – so extreme it can only be described as being born again or having a new life. It is a spiritual birth, a birth that is life-changing and so gratifying that it can only be by the love and power of God Himself.

Regeneration refers to a new birth, or rebirth, or the new nature of the believer.

Justification

Next is *dikaioo* the Greek word for justification. Justification is the act whereby an individual legal position has been changed from an alien of heaven to a citizen of heaven and into a new relationship with God the Father. It is an act of God's grace wherein He forgives our sins and accepts the believer as righteous or to be in right relationship with Him based on faith in Jesus Christ.[2]

Justification *has saved us* from the penalty of sin.

> "Therefore no one will be justified in His sight by works of the law. For the law merely brings awareness of sin. But now, apart from the law, the righteousness of God has been revealed, as attested by the Law and the Prophets. And this righteousness from God comes through faith in Jesus Christ to all who believe. There is

no distinction, for all have sinned and fall short of the glory of God, and are justified freely by His grace through the redemption that is in Christ Jesus. God presented Him as the atoning sacrifice through faith in His blood, in order to demonstrate His righteousness, because in His forbearance He had passed over the sins committed beforehand. He did this to demonstrate His righteousness at the present time, so as to be just and to justify the one who has faith in Jesus. Where, then, is boasting? It is excluded. On what principle? On that of works? No, but on that of faith. For we maintain that a man is justified by faith apart from works of the law. Is God the God of Jews only? Is He not the God of Gentiles too? Yes, of Gentiles too, since there is only one God, who will justify the circumcised by faith and the uncircumcised through that same faith. Do we, then, nullify the law by this faith? Certainly not! Instead, we uphold the law" (Romans 3:20-31 BSB).

Justification deals with our past. Here the Bible tells us, "for all have sinned and fallen short of the glory of God," and we are justified freely by His grace through the redemption that came by Christ Jesus. God dealt with our sin in the ultimate and most intimate way; He presented Jesus as a sacrifice of atonement. God did this to demonstrate His justice, wherein He pardoned all our sins and adopted us as children unto Himself (we receive legal sonship). This is only because of the righteousness of Jesus that is imputed to us by faith alone.

The short meaning of justification is, Just as if I had never sinned!

Salvation and Sanctification

Soteria is the Greek word that has these meanings: rescue, safety, deliver, health, save, saving and salvation. Salvation means the full deliverance of something or someone from impending danger, and this is what Jesus Christ fulfilled for all believers through His death, burial, and resurrection.

The Bible teaches us that salvation is threefold:

- First, salvation is nearly always by blood; Hebrews 9:22 (NIV) tells us, "In fact, the law requires that nearly everything be cleansed with blood, and without the shedding of blood there is no forgiveness."

- Second, salvation is always through the person of Jesus; Acts 4:12 (KJV) states, "Neither is there salvation in any other: for there is none other name under heaven given among men, whereby we must be saved"; and 1 Thessalonians 5:9 (NIV) says, "For God did not appoint us to suffer wrath but to receive salvation through our Lord Jesus Christ."

- Third, salvation is always by grace; 1 Corinthians 1:3 (BSB) says, "Grace and peace to you from God our Father and the Lord Jesus Christ; and Romans 1:7 (NIV) states, "To all in Rome who are loved by God and called to be his holy people: Grace and peace to you from God our Father and from the Lord Jesus Christ."

Sanctification is the process in salvation by which God conforms the life and character of the believer into that of Jesus through the Holy Spirit.[3]

It's very important that you clearly understand your salvation and sanctification. Sanctification occurs in the present age or period in which we are now living, and sanctification is saving us from the power of sin.

However, when we receive sanctification through Jesus the Lord and Savior, it is in three forms: instantly, positionally, and progressively:

- The first form is instantly: I AM – A New Creature. The Bible tells us in 2 Corinthians 5:17 (BSB), "Therefore if anyone is in Christ, he is a new creation. The old has passed away. Behold, the new has come!"

- The second form of sanctification is our position in Christ Jesus. Positional: we have been raised up with Christ – "Since you have been raised to new life with Christ, set your sights on the realities of heaven, where Christ sits in the place of honor at God's right hand" (Colossians 3:1 NLT) and seated in heavenly places – "For he raised us from the dead along with Christ and seated us with him in the heavenly realms because we are united with Christ Jesus" (Ephesians 2:6 NLT).

- The third level is progressive; Paul tells us in Philippians 3:14 (NIV), "I press on toward the goal to win the prize for which God has called me heavenward in Christ Jesus." The progressive part of our sanctification is a person's response to the call and command of God.

Therefore, in our sanctification we are instantly made holy, we are positionally holy, and we are progressively pursuing holiness.

In the section which I call "Paul's New Attitude," you will gain a better understanding of our progressive stage (pursuing holiness) and this is where I got the title for this book, In the Pursuit of Holiness.

The short answer to the meaning of sanctification is this: I am saved from the power of sin!

Note: Justification is an act, while sanctification is a work. Justification is the means, while sanctification is the end. Justification removes the guilt and the penalty of sin, while sanctification removes the growth and power of sin. Justification works for us, while Sanctification works in us. Justification declares us to be righteous, while sanctification makes us righteous. Justification is the past, and sanctification is the present.

Glorification

The word glorification is not used in the Hebrew Old Testament or the Greek New Testament, but glorification is communicated as *doxazo* in in its verb form and *doxa* in the noun form, meaning the act of glorifying or the state of being glorified. It is the ultimate state of every believer, though it has not yet occurred. It is the *future* for Christians that after death, the mortal bodies of Christians will be transformed into eternal physical bodies like that of Christ Jesus.

- "And if children, then heirs—heirs of God and joint heirs with Christ, if indeed we suffer with Him, that we may also be glorified together" (Romans 8:17 NKJV).

- "Moreover, whom He predestined, these He also called; whom He called, these He also justified; and whom He justified, these He also glorified" (Romans 8:30 NKJV).

- "Beloved, now we are children of God, and what we will be has not yet been revealed. We know that when He appears, we will be like Him, for we will see Him as He is" (1 John 3:2 BLB).

- "So will it be with the resurrection of the dead. The body that is sown is perishable, it is raised imperishable; it is sown in dishonor, it is raised in glory; it is sown in weakness, it is raised in power; it is sown a natural body, it is raised a spiritual body. If there is a natural body, there is also a spiritual body" (1 Corinthians 15:42-44 NIV).

The glorification period will be after the completion of the sanctification process. Our bodies will be transformed, and the old nature will be eliminated forever.

Glorification says that I will one day be saved from the presence of sin!

Therefore, we find that the words regeneration, justification, sanctification and glorification are of great significance in the life of the Christian. First the word regeneration refers to a new birth or rebirth or the new nature of the believer by the Holy Spirit, so we are presently holy. The word justification means that we have been saved us from the penalty of our sins. Sanctification means that Christians are saved and are being saved from the power of sin. And the word glorification tells us that one day Christians will be saved us from the presence of sin.

In the book of Philippians Paul gives us a great example of his understanding of our progressive or pursuing stage of holiness, which I call Paul's New Attitude.

As we look at Paul's letter to the church at Philippi, we can see the new attitude and understanding he has about his present and future salvation or sanctification that is found in our Lord Jesus Christ only.

Paul's New Attitude

"Yes, everything else is worthless when compared with the infinite value of knowing Christ Jesus my Lord. For his sake I have discarded everything else, counting it all as garbage, so that I could gain Christ and become one with him. I no longer count on my own righteousness through obeying the law; rather, I become righteous through faith in Christ. For God's way of making us right with himself depends on faith. I want to know Christ and experience the mighty power that raised him from the dead. I want to suffer with him, sharing in his death, so that one way or another I will experience the resurrection from the dead! I don't mean to say that I have already achieved these things or that I have already reached perfection. But I press on to possess that perfection for which Christ Jesus first possessed me. No, dear brothers and sisters, I have not achieved it, but I focus on this one thing: Forgetting the past and looking forward to what lies ahead, I press on to reach the end of the race and receive the heavenly prize for which God, through Christ Jesus, is calling us. Let all who are spiritually mature agree on these things. If you disagree on some point, I believe God will make it plain to you. But we must hold on to the progress we have already made. Dear brothers and sisters, pattern your lives after mine, and learn from those who follow our example. For I have told you often before, and I say it again with tears in my eyes, that there are many whose conduct shows they are really enemies of the cross of Christ. They are headed for destruction. Their god is their appetite, they brag about shameful things, and they think only about this life here on earth. But we are citizens of heaven, where the Lord Jesus Christ lives. And we are eagerly waiting for him to return as our Savior. He will take our weak mortal bodies and change them into glorious bodies like his own, using the same power with which he will bring everything under his control" (Philippians 3:8-21 NLT).

The first thing Paul lets us know is that our righteousness is through faith in Christ Jesus!

"And be found in Him, not having my own righteousness which is of the Law, but that which is through faith from Christ, the righteousness of God on the basis of faith" (Philippians 3:9 BLB).

"Isaiah tells us, "For all of us have become like one who is unclean, And all our righteous deeds are like a filthy garment; And all of us wither like a leaf, And our wrongdoings, like the wind, take us away" (Isaiah 64:6 NASB).

Second, Paul points out his goal and his goal is clear – to attain the resurrection. In Philippians 3:10-11 (BSB), Paul states, "I want to know Christ and the power of His resurrection and the fellowship of His sufferings, being conformed to Him in His death, and so, somehow, to attain to the resurrection from the dead." He may have understood the resurrection better than anyone else because in his second letter to the Corinth's, he states that he was caught up to paradise. He heard inexpressible things; things that man is not permitted to tell.

The third point Paul makes is that he has not yet obtained the highest level of holiness, but he is pressing to take hold of it. This word "press" comes from the Greek work dioko which means to pursue, ensue, follow after, and press forward. Paul paints a picture of himself straining with every ounce of strength, running to complete the race and determined not to fall short.

"Not that I have already obtained all this, or have already been made perfect, but I press on to take hold of that for which Christ Jesus took hold of me. Brothers, I do not consider myself yet to have taken hold of it. But one thing I do: Forgetting what is behind and straining toward what is ahead, I press on toward the goal to win the prize of God's heavenly calling in Christ Jesus" (Philippians 3:12-14 BSB).

Here is where most Christians fall short in their spiritual growth. Most Christians do not understand that the goal of the believer is to be Christ-like and that the Christian's life is a persistent pursuit of Christ-likeness (Holiness). The Bible tells us that "For those God foreknew, He also predestined to be conformed to the image of His Son, so that He would be the firstborn among many brothers" (Romans 8:29 BSB), God's ultimate purpose is to conform our lives into that of Jesus Christ. We must make it our goal as Paul did, to pursue holiness tenaciously and progressively in order to attain it. Paul also refers to our ultimate salvation and glorification in God's presence and the receiving of our rewards.

Note: This is where I get the title for this book "In the Pursuit of Holiness." Paul understood the third level of salvation and our sanctification process. He understood that we are to be pursuing the things of God the Father with our minds, bodies, souls and strength which Jesus Christ taught and modeled for us.

Fourthly, Paul was determined to share the Gospel with as many as he could, to help them understand the proclamation of the biblical and historical person and works of Jesus Christ. With the grace of God, he would persuade men and women all over the world to put their trust in Jesus Christ exclusively as their only means of salvation as he had done.

"Let those of us who are mature think this way, and if in anything you think otherwise, God will reveal that also to you. Only let us hold true to what we have attained. Brothers, join in imitating me, and keep your eyes on those who walk according to the example you have in us" (Philippians 3:15-17 ESV).

Finally, Paul warns about the false teachers. He called them enemies of the cross and he points out their destination. Then he tells us that our citizenship is in heaven and we are strangers here on this earth. He also reiterates the glorification period in which our bodies will be transformed into glorious bodies like Jesus.

"as I have often told you before, and now say again even with tears: Many live as enemies of the cross of Christ. Their end is destruction, their god is their belly, and their glory is in their shame. Their minds are set on earthly things. But our citizenship is in heaven, and we eagerly await a Savior from there, the Lord Jesus Christ, who, by the power that enables Him to subject all things to Himself, will transform our lowly bodies to be like His glorious body (Philippians 3:18-21 BSB)."

PRAYER:

Father God, as I study Your Word, please empower me through the Holy Spirit to understand Your truths. Please help me to grow from milk to meat in my salvation, that others may see the work of the Holy Spirit in my life and that Your name would be glorified. In Jesus' name – AMEN

Reflection Time:

1. How have We received Regeneration, Justification and Sanctification?

    _____
    _____
    _____
    _____
    _____
    _____
    _____
    _____
    _____

2. In your own words explain Regeneration:

    _____
    _____
    _____
    _____
    _____
    _____
    _____
    _____
    _____

3. In your own words explain Justification:

    _____
    _____
    _____
    _____
    _____
    _____
    _____
    _____
    _____

4. In your own words explain Sanctification:

    _____
    _____
    _____
    _____
    _____
    _____
    _____
    _____
    _____
    _____

5. In your own words explain Glorification:

    _____
    _____
    _____
    _____
    _____
    _____
    _____
    _____
    _____
    _____

6. How can you apply what you have learned in this chapter to your personal life?

    _____
    _____
    _____
    _____
    _____
    _____
    _____
    _____
    _____
    _____

7. Knowing this information will help me . . .

_____

_____

_____

_____

_____

_____

_____

_____

_____

"It's through the life, death, burial, and the resurrection of Jesus Christ that we have received sanctification, regeneration, justification and glorification and outside of a relationship with Him there is no salvation."

"This is the gospel of Jesus Christ!"

Chapter Two

"What does Jesus want most from me?"

"A Personal Relationship"

"Now when he saw the crowds, he went up on a mountainside and sat down. His disciples came to him, and he began to teach them" (Matthew 5:1-2 NIV).

What does Jesus want most from me? The answer to this question is one most Christians don't understand or know. Some may say that He wants Christians to be a good people, to follow His Commandments . . . So then what is your definition for being good, and what are His Commandments? In most of today's churches we find there is a lot of misunderstanding about what God/Jesus really wants from us. The answer is simple: He wants a relationship with you! Jesus tells us:

> "'... You shall love the Lord your God with all your heart and with all your soul and with all your mind. This is the great and first commandment. And a second is like it: You shall love your neighbor as yourself" (Matthew 22:37-39 ESV).

If you were to ask Jesus what He truly wants from us . . . He would say relationship, relationship, relationship! He wants us to love Him as much as He loves us!

As we look throughout the Bible, we find Jesus and the Apostles pointing out the principles of what a true relationship means through their messages and writings. More importantly, they showed the principles of relationship through their actions so that we may truly understand what God/Jesus wants from us.

If you were sincere when you asked Jesus Christ to come into your life, you can be sure that your relationship with God is secure. To know Jesus Christ as our Lord and Savior is the most exciting relationship anyone can ever have. It is the beginning of life with an all-loving and all-powerful God.

As we grow more mature in our spiritual lives, we will become more intimate with Him in our personal relationship and our faith will grow to the point where we can share our deepest secrets with Him. However, Jesus already knows everything about us, but when we choose to tell him about the hidden things deep inside of us this will show him that we truly trust him.

Jesus wants to lead and protect us every day through this evil world with His truth, His mercy, His grace and His love. He said, "I am the way, the truth, and the life" (John 14:6 KJV).

First, we must ask and answer the age-old question, why did God make us? The answer mostly given by people is that God wanted more friends. To have more friends is not the answer because He had the Son and the Holy Spirit; in addition, He created millions of angels.

The book of Genesis begins by letting us know that God is a creative being, and it gives Him pleasure to create.

The Purpose of Man

In the book of Genesis, we find that in the beginning God created the heavens and the earth, day and night, all the animals on our planet, and that the culmination of His creation was the creation of MAN:

- "Then God said, "Let us make man in our image" (Genesis 1:26 ESV).

- "Then the LORD God formed man from the dust of the ground and breathed the breath of life into his nostrils, and the man became a living being" (Genesis 2:7 BSB).

- "Male and female He created them, and He blessed them. And in the day, they were created, He called them "man"" (Genesis 5:2 BSB).

Because of this divine action of God, man has both a material and a spiritual nature. The spiritual nature of man reflects being created in God's image, this means man has a "spirit and soul and body."

The Bible tells us that the first purpose for God's creation us is that we might know Him, glorify Him and enjoy Him forever! God made us to show forth His goodness and to share in His everlasting glory in heaven.

- "...that in everything God may be glorified through Jesus Christ" (1 Peter 4:11 ESV).

- ". . . and so we will always be with the Lord" (1 Thessalonians 4:17 ESV).

God is also a personal being, and it gives Him pleasure to have other beings He can have a genuine relationship with. Therefore, one purpose and reason God created man was to fellowship with Him.

Let's see what Jesus has to say about the type of relationship He wants to have with us, he says to us:

"You shall love the Lord your God with all your heart, with all your soul, and with all your mind.' This is the first and great commandment.

And the second is like it: 'You shall love your neighbor as yourself" (Matthew 22:37-39 NKJV).

This type of relationship is NOT about doing things, religious activities, or by keeping a list of rules. It's NOT about just reading our Bible every day, remembering scripture verses, or having quiet time (all of these are good and should be done). This relationship is all about loving a Holy God/Jesus and loving other people through relationships.

To the person that says relationship is about keeping His Commandments; Jesus says that keeping His commands is a statement of our love for Him. He stated:

> "Whoever has my commandments and keeps them, he it is who loves me. And he who loves me will be loved by my Father, and I will love him and manifest myself to him" (John 14:21 ESV).

We must all ask ourselves these important questions: Do I really have a true relationship with God/Jesus?" Am I obedient to His commands based on love?

The second purpose and reason God created man was to serve and worship Him. In the Book of Exodus chapter twenty we find the Ten Commandments God gave us through Moses. When we take a close look at the Ten Commandments, we find that the first four commands pertain to our relationship with God, and the last six pertain to our relationships with other humans.

> "And God spoke all these words, saying, "I am the LORD your God, who brought you out of the land of Egypt, out of the house of slavery. "You shall have no other gods before me. "You shall not make for yourself a carved image, or any likeness of anything that is in heaven above, or that is in the earth beneath, or that is in the water under the earth. You shall not bow down to them or serve them, for I the LORD your God am a jealous God, visiting the iniquity of the fathers on the children to the

third and the fourth generation of those who hate me, but showing steadfast love to thousands of those who love me and keep my commandments. "You shall not take the name of the LORD your God in vain, for the LORD will not hold him guiltless who takes his name in vain. "Remember the Sabbath day, to keep it holy" (Exodus 20:1-8 ESV).

This also lines up with what Jesus said to Satan in the desert during his temptation in Matthew 4:1-11; Mark 1:12-13; and Luke 4:1-13. Jesus said to him, "Away from me, Satan! For it is written: 'Worship the Lord your God, and serve him only.'"

"Fear the LORD your God, serve him only and take your oaths in his name. Do not follow other gods, the gods of the peoples around you; for the LORD your God, who is among you, is a jealous God and his anger will burn against you, and he will destroy you from the face of the land. Do not test the LORD your God as you did at Massah" (Deuteronomy 6:13-16 NIV).

The third reason and purpose God created man was to live eternally with Him. We find that the Bible tells us consistently that Life was intended to be lived eternally – forever with God.

- "You have made known to me the path of life; You will fill me with joy in Your presence, with eternal pleasures at Your right hand" (Psalm 16:11 BSB).

- Jesus said, "And I give unto them eternal life; and they shall never perish, neither shall any man pluck them out of my hand" (John 10:28 KJV).

- "And this is the testimony, that God gave us eternal life, and this life is in his Son" (1 John 5:11 ESV).

- "And we know that the Son of God has come, and he has given us understanding so that we can know the true God. And now we live in fellowship with the true God because we live in fellowship with his Son, Jesus Christ. He is the only true God, and he is eternal life" (1 John 5:20 NLT).

- "According to the eternal purpose that He accomplished in Christ Jesus our Lord. In Him and through faith in Him we may enter God's presence with boldness and confidence" (Ephesians 3:11-12 BSB).

"But" ... we all know the story in Genesis chapter three, how sin came into the world. Satan through a serpent managed to influence Adam and Eve to disobey God the Father. When Adam and Eve ate from the Tree of the Knowledge of Good and Evil, they were actually rejecting God's Lordship for what they thought was their own. Satan told them that if they ate from that particular tree, they would be better off and could decide for themselves independently of God. All Christians know now that is not true; nothing, absolutely nothing can live independently of God.

Adam and Eve's disobedience actually switched their allegiance from God the Father unto Satan. By their disobedience all human descendants of Adam are born with a sin nature causing sickness, pain, suffering, wars, death and all the other problems we face. This act of human rebellion against God created a broken relationship with a Holy God.

This is why Jesus had to come from heaven to earth. He came to fix the broken relationship between God and man. The Bible tells us that He is the propitiation for our sins, not for ours only, but for the sins of the whole world. This word propitiation means an action directed towards God, seeking to change God's wrath to favor. This is what Jesus did; He paid the Penalty for Atonement, and He came to restore our broken relationship with God.[4]

Paul explains to us that we have all received death through Adam and we received Life through Jesus Christ.

> "Therefore, just as sin entered the world through one man, and death through sin, so also death was passed on to all men, because all sinned. For sin was in the world before the law was given; but sin is not taken into account when there is no law. Nevertheless, death

reigned from Adam until Moses, even over those who did not sin in the way that Adam transgressed. He is a pattern of the One to come. But the gift is not like the trespass. For if the many died by the trespass of the one man, how much more did God's grace and the gift that came by the grace of the one man, Jesus Christ, abound to the many! Again, the gift is not like the result of the one man's sin: The judgment that followed one sin brought condemnation, but the gift that followed many trespasses brought justification. For if, by the trespass of the one man, death reigned through that one man, how much more will those who receive an abundance of grace and of the gift of righteousness reign in life through the one man, Jesus Christ! So then, just as one trespass brought condemnation for all men, so also one act of righteousness brought justification and life for all men. For just as through the disobedience of the one man the many were made sinners, so also through the obedience of the one man the many will be made righteous. The law came in so that the trespass would increase; but where sin increased, grace increased all the more, so that, just as sin reigned in death, so also grace might reign through righteousness to bring eternal life through Jesus Christ our Lord" (Romans 5:12-21 BSB).

This is why it is so important that we have a relationship with Jesus. He tells us: "I am the way, and the truth, and the life. No one comes to the Father except through me" (John 14:6 (ESV).

- Jesus is "The Way" – He is the only way to having a love relationship with the Father. And He demonstrated how we should live and treat others.

- Jesus is "The Truth" – He demonstrates for us true love and compassion, and the truth of the Gospel by which we all should live.

- Jesus is "The Life" – He is the giver and creator of all life. He came to give us a quality life, abundant life, and eternal life.

Understand that Jesus is the Life, the giver of life, and the all-powerful creator of life. He says to us: "I have come that they may have life, and that they may have it more abundantly" (John 10:10 NKJV). Jesus wants to give us a life of peace, a life of rest, and a life of joy. But it is available to us only if we accept him on a personal level. Jesus tells us in the book of Matthew, "Come to me, all you who are weary and burdened, and I will give you rest. Take my yoke upon you and learn from me, for I am gentle and humble in heart, and you will find rest for your souls." Here Jesus says to us, "Come to me," let's have an intimate relationship."[5]

The Apostle Paul understood this when he said, "For I am not ashamed of the gospel, for it is the power of God for salvation to everyone who believes, to the Jew first and also to the Greek. For in it the righteousness of God is revealed from faith for faith, as it is written, "The righteous shall live by faith" (Romans 1:16-17 ESV). Here, Paul put his faith in Jesus, and this allowed their relationship to grow.

When I say personal level, I mean our relationship with Jesus should be an intimate knowledge of who He is. For example, I can say I know the President of the United States of America, but the truth is I only know some facts about him. The real truth is that only his wife and the people most close to him have an intimate personal relationship with him! This is how some Christians view their relationship with Jesus! They only know what they heard about Him in church and from others, and they never come to know Him in a most intimate and personal way.

The Bible points out to us how Jesus modeled intimate and personal relationships throughout time as He fellowshipped with people. In the book of Luke chapter ten, Jesus and His disciples had been invited to the home of Mary and Martha. In their home, He pointed out an act of great importance: spending time with Him with an open mind and heart open to the Word of God, with an attitude of worship and fellowship.

> "As they traveled along; Jesus entered a village where a woman named Martha welcomed Him into her home. She had a sister named Mary, who sat at the Lord's feet listening to His message. But Martha was distracted by

all the preparations to be made. She came to Jesus and said, "Lord, do You not care that my sister has left me to serve alone? Tell her to help me!" "Martha, Martha," the Lord replied, "you are worried and upset about many things. But only one thing is necessary. Mary has chosen the good portion, and it will not be taken away from her" (Luke 10:38-42 BSB).

We also find that in some of Jesus' last prayers (recorded in John chapter fourteen and John chapter seventeen), He expressed His desire to maintain His relationship with His disciples and all that put their trust and faith in Him here on earth and in heaven.

Jesus' Intercessory Prayer

"But now I am coming to You; and I am saying these things while I am in the world, so that they may have My joy fulfilled within them. I have given them Your word and the world has hated them; for they are not of the world, just as I am not of the world. I am not asking that You take them out of the world, but that You keep them from the evil one. They are not of the world, just as I am not of the world. Sanctify them by the truth; Your word is truth. As You sent Me into the world, I have also sent them into the world. For them I sanctify Myself, so that they too may be sanctified by the truth. I am not asking on behalf of them alone, but also on behalf of those who will believe in Me through their message, that all of them may be one, as You, Father, are in Me, and I am in You. May they also be in Us, so that the world may believe that You sent Me. I have given them the glory You gave Me, so that they may be one as We are one— I in them and You in Me—that they may be perfectly united, so that the world may know that You sent Me and have loved them just as You have loved Me. Father, I want those You have given Me to be with Me where I am, that they may see the glory You gave Me because You loved Me before the foundation of the world. Righteous Father, although the world has not known You, I know You, and they know that You sent Me. And I have made Your name known to them and will continue to make it known, so that the love You have for Me may be in them, and I in them" (John 17:13-26 BSB).

Jesus' Comforts His Disciples

"Let not your hearts be troubled. Believe in God; believe also in me. In my Father's house are many rooms. If it were not so, would I have told you that I go to prepare a place for you? And if I go and prepare a place for you, I will come again and will take you to myself, that where I am you may be also. And you know the way to where I am going" (John14:1-4 ESV).

Remember, Jesus came to restore the broken relationship between man and God the Father so we may live, worship, and fellowship with Him for eternity because we were created to have an intimate relationship with Him.

"For God so loved the world, that he gave his only Son, that whoever believes in him should not perish but have eternal life" (John 3:16 ESV).

To develop a relationship with Jesus Christ, starts by praying to Him and by reading His Word. When we pray, we are talking to God and when we read our Bibles, He is talking to us. A relationship with Jesus is the most important decision we will ever make. It is the decision to accept or reject Him as Lord and Savior. It is your most important calling now!

What does Jesus want most from you and me? It is not what the world thinks. The world believe that Christianity is based on a set of rules, a lot of dos and don'ts. This is so farther from the truth. Jesus wants a relationship with every one of us!" He wants us to love Him, and God the Father with all our heart and with all our soul and with our entire mind; And for each of us to Love our neighbor as ourselves.

Here in this chapter Jesus shows us the heart of God by revealing His eternal purpose for man ... a love relationship! God loves us, and His greatest desire is to have an intimate relationship with each, and every one of us. He does not want religion or religious people; He wants a relationship!

PRAYER:

Lord God I pray that you would reveal Yourself to me in a powerful way. I want to know You at the highest lever a human can know a Holy God. Farther I open the door of my heart to You Jesus and I remove all locks. Lord, help me through the Holy Spirit to grow closer to You and further from this world. Lord as I fellowship with You, please help me to remember that my relationship with you is the most important relationship there is. In Jesus' name – AMEN

Reflection Time:

1. We must all ask ourselves this important question: "Do I really have a true relationship with God/Jesus?" How would you answer this and why?

   _____
   _____
   _____
   _____
   _____
   _____
   _____
   _____
   _____

2. Am I obedient to His commands based on _____? Please explain your answer.

   _____
   _____
   _____
   _____
   _____
   _____
   _____
   _____

3. Why did Jesus have to come from heaven to earth?

   _____
   _____
   _____
   _____
   _____
   _____
   _____
   _____

4. What steps will you commit to take to create a better relationship with Jesus?

_____

_____

_____

_____

_____

_____

_____

_____

_____

_____

5. Who will be the person that will hold you accountable in this area?

_____

_____

_____

_____

_____

_____

_____

_____

_____

_____

6. How can you apply what you've learned in this chapter to your personal life?

_____

_____

_____

_____

_____

_____

_____

_____

Jesus wants a Relationship with you!"

"Behold, I stand at the door and knock. If anyone hears my voice and opens the door, I will come in to him and eat with him, and he with me" (Revelation 3:20 ESV).

As you can see, there is no knob on the outside of the door, it's on the inside; you must open the door of your heart.

"Jesus is at the door; will you let Him in?"

Chapter Three

"Totally Surrendering All"

Making Jesus your Lord and Savior"

"Blessed are those who hunger and thirst for righteousness, For they shall be filled" (Matthew 5:6 NKJV).

Now that we understand that the first thing God wants from us is a relationship, what does He want from us next? There is one thing most Christians have not done, and that is to totally surrender their entire lives to Jesus. Today's statistics tell us that only one out of every ten people in the church have totally surrendered their lives to God.[6] This means that 90% of the congregation does not understand that they should be pursuing holiness and seeking an intimate relationship with the Lord Jesus.[7]

Totally surrendering to God/Jesus may very well be the biggest component that is missing in our churches today, and it may be the reason we have so little power in our lives.[8]

So . . . be honest . . . how many of us could truly say we have totally surrendered ourselves to God; meaning, every area of our lives?

Let's look at what Jesus has to say about surrendering our lives to God the Father.

> "Then Jesus told his disciples, "If anyone would come after me, let him deny himself and take up his cross and follow me. For whoever would save his life will lose it, but whoever loses his life for my sake will find it. For what will it profit a man if he gains the whole world and forfeits his soul? Or what shall a man give in return for his soul? For the Son of Man is going to come with his angels in the glory of his Father, and then he will repay each person according to what he has done" (Matthew 16:24-27 ESV).

Understand what Jesus is saying, He said that we must be truly committed to following Him with the understanding that there is no turning back, even if it leads to death. His disciples understood exactly what Jesus meant when He said, "Whoever wants to be my disciple must deny themselves and take up their cross and follow Me." Because crucifixion was common in their day, Jesus needed them to understand what following Him might cost them. He pointed out that real discipleship entails the real commitment of pledging your entire life to Him in service.

Next, Jesus teaches us that if we value our physical lives more than our spiritual lives, we run the risk of losing out on eternal life. He wants us to understand that the more we hold on to the physical (flesh, material possessions, money), we will die spiritually; our focus will turn inward, and we will not fulfill our purpose.

Once we come to the understanding of surrendering our lives to God, we will then discover the real purpose for our lives.

It all comes down to control! The question we must ask ourselves is this: Will I surrender control of my life to the one that created it (Jesus)? For the Bible tells us ". . . for You created all things; by Your will they exist and came to be" (Revelation 4:11 BSB). We also found that Jesus uses His creation to teach us that the surrendering of our lives to His will lead to a blessed life. Jesus states:

> "Very truly I tell you, unless a kernel of wheat falls to the ground and dies, it remains only a single seed. But if it dies, it produces many seeds. Anyone who loves their life will lose it, while anyone who hates their life in this world will keep it for eternal life" (John 12:24-25 NIV).

Here, Jesus is telling us that if we hold on to our lives, wanting to remain in control, we will lose our chance at eternal life. But if we surrender, we will gain eternal life.

Jesus uses a kernel of wheat, a small seed, to help us understand physical and spiritual laws.

First, what is a seed? A seed is stored energy. The seed must go into the ground and it must surrender to the elements (the soil, water, and sun) to grow and bring forth life. The seed always surrenders; the seed is never in control. So here with a small seed we find that even nature/creation can teach us about surrendering and not resisting God's control.

This is also a picture of the sacrifice Christ Jesus made for the sins of all mankind. He was buried to show His power over death and His resurrection proves that He has the power of eternal life.

Jesus Christ is the greatest example of surrendering there has ever been! The Bible tells us He surrendered even before He came to earth. In His incarnation Jesus voluntarily became a man. Jesus obediently and submissively surrendered to the Father's will. It's important to note He never gave up His deity to become a man (as Jesus is fully God and fully man), but He abstained or set aside His power and glory for a time. Jesus surrendered His Life as a sacrifice (sin offering) for our sins.

- "For you know the grace of our Lord Jesus Christ, that though He was rich, yet for your sakes He became poor, so that you through His poverty might become rich" (2 Corinthians 8:9 BSB).

- "Who, being in the form of God, did not consider it robbery to be equal with God, but made Himself of no reputation, taking the form of a bondservant, and coming in the likeness of men" (Philippians 2:6-7 NKJV).

- "The Word (Jesus) became flesh and made his dwelling among us. We have seen his glory, the glory of the One and Only, who came from the Father, full of grace and truth" (John 1:14 BSB).

- "For what the law was powerless to do in that it was weakened by the flesh, God did by sending His own Son in the likeness of sinful man, as an offering for sin. He thus condemned sin in the flesh" (Romans 8:3 BSB).

- "For this reason, he had to be made like his brothers in every way, in order that he might become a merciful and faithful high priest in service to God, and that he might make atonement for the sins of the people" (Hebrews 2:17 BSB).

The Bible also shows us that Jesus surrendered to the Father even in His prayer life. We find this in the gospels of Matthew, Mark, and Luke where Jesus and His disciples had eaten the Passover meal and they had come to the place called Gethsemane which means olive press. Here the Bible states that Jesus prayed three times to the Father about surrendering to the Father's will:

"At that time Jesus went with His disciples to a place called Gethsemane, and He told them, "Sit here while I go over there and pray." He took with Him Peter and the two sons of Zebedee and began to be sorrowful and deeply distressed. Then He said to them, "My soul is consumed with sorrow to the point of death. Stay here and keep watch with Me." Going a little farther, He fell facedown and prayed, "My Father, if it is possible, let this cup pass from Me. Yet not as I will, but as You will." Then Jesus returned to the disciples and found them sleeping. "Were you not able to keep watch with Me for one hour?" He asked Peter. "Watch and pray so that you will not enter into temptation. For the spirit is willing, but the body is weak." A second time He went away and prayed, "My Father, if this cup cannot pass unless I drink it, may Your will be done." And again Jesus returned and found them sleeping—for their eyes were heavy. So He left them and went away once more and prayed a third time, saying the same thing" (Matthew 26:36-44 BSB).

Not only did Jesus surrender to the Father's will, He called all Christians to surrender their lives and will to God the Father also.

- "Then Jesus said to His disciples, "If anyone desires to come after Me, let him deny himself, and take up his cross, and follow Me. For whoever desires to save his life will lose it, but whoever loses his life for My sake will find it" (Matthew 16:24-25 NKJV).

- "Anyone who loves his father or mother more than Me is not worthy of Me; anyone who loves his son or daughter more than Me is not worthy of Me; and anyone who does not take up his cross and follow Me is not worthy of Me" (Matthew 10:37-38 BSB).

We find here that all Christians are called to follow the Lord Jesus Christ by imitating Him in every way. To take up our cross means to identify with Christ. We must die to our selfish desires and follow the life of Christ Jesus by obeying His Commands.

We also find that the Apostle Paul understood what it meant to surrender to the will of God. He wrote to the church in Rome and explained it to them in the book of Romans. He started with the theology side; first, with "sin" in chapters 1, 2 and 3; "salvation" in chapters 3, 4 and 5; "sanctification" in chapters 6, 7 and 8; "sovereignty" in chapters 9, 10, and 11; "service" in chapters 12 through 14 (God, church, society, government, brethren); and his "desire and benediction" in chapters 15 and 16.

In Chapter 12 though chapter 14 Paul talks about how Christians should live their lives as a redeemed people in a sinful world. Paul tells us we should give or surrender ourselves to Jesus Christ as living sacrifices:

- "Do not present the parts of your body to sin as instruments of wickedness, but present yourselves to God as those who have been brought from death to life; and present the parts of your body to Him as instruments of righteousness" (Romans 6:13 BSB).

- "Don't you know that when you offer yourselves to someone to obey him as slaves, you are slaves to the one whom you obey--whether you are slaves to sin, which leads to death, or to obedience, which leads to righteousness" (Roman 6:16 NIV)?

- "I am using an example from everyday life because of your human limitations. Just as you used to offer yourselves as slaves to impurity and to ever-increasing wickedness, so now offer yourselves as slaves to righteousness leading to holiness" (Romans 6:19 NIV).

- "Don't you realize that your body is the temple of the Holy Spirit, who lives in you and was given to you by God? You do not belong to yourself, for God bought you with a high price. So, you must honor God with your body" (1 Corinthians 6:19-20 NLT).

- "I appeal to you therefore, brothers, by the mercies of God, to present your bodies as a living sacrifice, holy and acceptable to God, which is your spiritual worship" (Romans 12:1 ESV).

In Romans, Paul tells the church in Rome in the first eleven chapters about the foundation of the gospel, our salvation, and what is pleasing to God. After this chapter Paul spends the rest of this letter giving the church guidelines for living as redeemed people.

We know that offering sacrifices was an important part of the Jewish religion and other religions at that time. Paul wants the new followers of Jesus Christ to understand that animal sacrifices are not needed in order to please God. He would rather have each of us offer (surrender) ourselves in service to Him.

Paul is basically telling us, that based on what God has done for us at Calvary we should be willing to give back to Him. He says that all believers should be devoted (surrender) to God with everything we have for service and worship. This means we are to surrender all to God; our minds, our will, our emotions, our attitudes, our bodies and our souls. Anything less than our total devotion to a Holy God/Jesus is dishonoring and robs Him of His Glory.

The Bible also gives us a great example of people who refuse to surrender to Jesus and the consequences for not doing so. Such an example can be found in the book of Matthew Chapter Ten. This person I'm referring to is known in the Bible as the rich young ruler. In this passage, the young man was seeking the assurance of eternal life; however, Jesus points out to him that salvation is not obtained by doing good deeds (works) only. Here is the story:

Rich Young Ruler

"Just then a man came up to Jesus and inquired, "Teacher, what good thing must I do to obtain eternal life?" "Why do you ask Me about what is good?" Jesus replied. "There is only One who is good. If you want to enter life, keep the commandments." "Which ones?" the man asked. Jesus answered, "'Do not murder, do not commit adultery, do not steal, do not bear false witness, honor your father and mother, and love your neighbor as yourself.' "All these I have kept," said the young man. "What do I still lack?" Jesus told him, "If you want to be perfect, go, sell your possessions, and give to the poor, and you will have treasure in heaven. Then come, follow Me." When the young man heard this, he went away in sorrow, because he had great wealth. Then Jesus said to His disciples, "Truly I tell you, it is hard for a rich man to enter the kingdom of heaven. Again I tell you, it is easier for a camel to pass through the eye of a needle than for a rich man to enter the kingdom of God." When the disciples heard this, they were greatly astonished and asked, "Who then can be saved?" Jesus looked at them and said, "With man this is impossible, but with God all things are possible" (Matthew 19:16-26 BSB).

Now that you have read the passage, you see that the young man wanted eternal life but he was not willing to follow the steps to obtain eternal life. Let's look at what Jesus said to him: God alone is good (v16), keep God's commands (v17), surrender everything to God, and surrender to the Lordship of Jesus Christ (v21).

However, we are told that when the young man heard this, he went away sad, because he had great wealth. This young man was more in love with his riches than eternal life and we should learn from this young man that we will never get God's best unless we do it His way!

In First Kings Chapter Nineteen, we find one of the best examples of surrendering. Here we have the call of Elisha into the service of the Lord. The Bible states:

> "So, he departed from there and found Elisha the son of Shaphat while he was plowing, with twelve yoke of oxen in front of him, and he with the twelfth. And Elijah came over to him and threw his cloak on him. Then he left the oxen behind and ran after Elijah, and said, "Please let me kiss my father and my mother, then I will follow you." And he said to him, "Go back, for what have I done to you?" So he returned from following him, and took the pair of oxen and sacrificed them, and cooked their meat with the implements of the oxen, and gave it to the people and they ate. Then he got up and followed Elijah and served him." (1 Kings 19:19-21 NASB).

Here we find an ordinary man plowing in his father's fields when he receives the call to serve. We can see Elisha demonstrate his commitment by the burning of the plow and the sacrificing of the oxen. Elisha gave up his known way of life. He surrendered everything: his plans, his family, friends, job and his life, so he could be what God/Jesus wanted him to be.

Surrendering all is a very frightening and radical thing for anyone to do. Some may say that it's a lot for someone to give up, but if you think about it for a minute, what are you giving up? A life that is separated from a Holy God, is that what you want?

We should understand by now that God/Jesus wants us to trust Him with every area of our lives. He wants us to have faith in Him that He will take care of us. The problem is never with God/Jesus, it's with our lack of faith. The writer of the book of Hebrews states, ". . . without faith it is impossible to please Him, for he who comes to God must believe that He is, and that He is a rewarder of those who diligently seek Him" (Hebrews 11:6 NKJV). He also tells us to "Let us fix our eyes on Jesus, the author and perfecter of our faith, who for the joy set before Him endured the cross, scorning its shame, and sat down at the right hand of the throne of God" (Hebrews 12:2 BSB).

Yes, God/Jesus wants us to surrender everything to Him; mind, body, soul, and will. He wants to be our security. He wants to be the first name you call when trouble comes your way. Jesus wants to be the one you place your trust in, knowing he will keep you.

If you surrender to Him, He said that He would never leave us; never will He forsake us. He will never let us down because He is always faithful.

We must ask ourselves some tough questions:

- In my heart of hearts, have I really surrendered each and every area of my life to Christ Jesus?
- Have I only made Jesus my Savior and not my Lord? . . . Jesus must be both!

God loves YOU! He's has promised in His Word He would bless us in the heavenly realms with every spiritual blessing in Christ (Ephesians 1:3 NLT). He also said that He himself will go before us and will be with us, and He would never leave us nor forsake us (Deuteronomy 31:6, 8; Joshua 1:5; Hebrews 13:5 NKJV).

To follow Christ is not easy - it's costly. However, we find out in the Word of God that if we surrender to His will, then we will share in the Joy of the Lord throughout eternity.

PRAYER:

> Dear Lord God, please be the LORD of my life. Help me to surrender each and every area of my life to you Jesus, as my Lord and Savior. Help me see you each day in all that I do, all that I say, and in the way I respond to adversity. Lord Jesus I give you total control of my life, I'm completely yours. Do with me as you will, not my will, but Your will be done. In Jesus' name – AMEN

Reflection Time:

1. In my heart of hearts, have I surrendered each and every area of my life to Christ Jesus? What areas in my life am I holding on to and why?

   _____
   _____
   _____
   _____
   _____
   _____
   _____
   _____
   _____

2. Have I only made Jesus my Savior and not my Lord? Remember He must be both! Explain your answer!

   _____
   _____
   _____
   _____
   _____
   _____
   _____
   _____

3. What steps will you commit to taking to totally surrender every area of your life to God?

   _____
   _____
   _____
   _____
   _____
   _____
   _____
   _____

4. Who will be the person that will hold you accountable in this area?

    _____
    _____
    _____
    _____
    _____
    _____
    _____
    _____

5. How can you apply what you've learned in this chapter to your personal life?

    _____
    _____
    _____
    _____
    _____
    _____
    _____
    _____

Have you made Jesus Lord over your life?
Are you "all in" or are you holding back?
Will you give God what He wants most – **"All of YOU!"**

Chapter Four

"Separation from this World"

"Our citizenship is in Heaven"

For I tell you that unless your righteousness surpasses that of the Pharisees and the teachers of the law, you will certainly not enter the kingdom of heaven (Matthew 5:20 NIV).

Wow! What if Jesus told you these words? How would you respond? But thanks be to God, that our righteousness is found in Jesus Christ and not in ourselves (1 Corinthians 1:30 BLB; Philippians 3:9 BLB).

The Pharisees were some of the most respected people in that day and the Scribes were known for their expert knowledge of The Law. Here Jesus wants us to understand that He wants more than just some religious-acting, scripture-remembering people. He wants that "Be"-attitude which flows from an internal righteousness based on faith, not a mere external righteousness as the Pharisees and Scribes had. He wants our hearts to be turned from this worldly system back into His original purpose for us.

Back in Chapter One, we talked about sanctification. We understand that it comes from the verb sanctify. This word sanctify comes from the Greek word hagiazo, which means to be "separate" or to be "set apart." In the Bible, sanctification is generally related to the sovereign act of God by which He "sets apart" something or someone to accomplish His will.

In this chapter, I want you to understand that God has placed a calling on our lives and He wants us to separate from this world because He has given us all a purpose and a job to do.

Here are some questions you may be asking yourself which we will try to answer:

- How can a Christian be in this world, and not be a part of this world?

- How does a person come out from under this world's system and live separate?

One of the first things we must understand about the world is that people who love the world (meaning the things in the "world," money, sex, houses or cars) and not God, are not our friends. The world will hate you just because you are a Christians and it will love you if you are a non-Christian.

In Chapter Four of the book of Matthew and in Luke Chapter Four, we find Satan trying to tempt Jesus with the things of the world and its system, these same things are destined to destroy our lives. Satan's system is designed to get us to violate or disobey the commands of God which would give Satan power over whoever submits to his temptation. Matthew Chapter Four also points out to us there is a real spiritual battle going on against Satan and this world's system.

However, Jesus also teaches and demonstrates for us how to be in the world but not of the world, and He shows us how to have victory over this world's temptations.[9]

The Temptation of Jesus

"Then Jesus was led by the Spirit into the desert to be tempted by the devil. After fasting forty days and forty nights, he was hungry. The tempter came to him and said, "If you are the Son of God, tell these stones to become bread." Jesus answered, "It is written: 'Man does not live on bread alone, but on every word, that comes from the mouth of God.'" Then the devil took him to the holy city and had him stand on the highest point of the temple. "If you are the Son of God," he said, "throw yourself down. For it is written:" 'He will command his angels concerning you, and they will lift you up in their hands, so that you will not strike your foot against a stone.'" Jesus answered him, "It is also written: 'Do not put the Lord your God to the test.'" Again, the devil took him to a very high mountain and showed him all the kingdoms of the world and their splendor. "All this I will give you," he said, "if you will bow down and worship me." Jesus said to him, "Away from me, Satan! For it is written: 'Worship the Lord your God, and serve him only.'" Then the devil left him, and angels came and attended him" (Matthew 4:1-11 NIV).

Let's look closely at this encounter between Jesus and Satan, the worldly ways Satan tricks or tempts all of mankind, and the obedience of Jesus to the Word of God in action.

The First Temptation:

- Satan stated, "If you are the Son of God, tell these stones to become bread" (v3). This temptation of Satan was to turn Jesus' spiritual nature into a means of satisfying His physical need without first finding out the will of God; therefore, he would be doing the will of the devil. However, Jesus turns to the Word of God and quotes Deuteronomy 8:3 (NASB), "It is written: 'Man shall not live on bread alone, but man shall live on everything that comes out of the mouth of the LORD.'"

- This temptation attempts to try to satisfy your physical needs outside of God's purpose and will. This is the "lust of the flesh."

The Second Temptation:

- The devil took him (Jesus) to the holy city and had him stand on the highest point of the temple and said, "If you are the Son of God," he said, "throw yourself down" (v5-6). The first temptation was a physical test, now the second temptation was a spiritual test; Satan tries to tempt Jesus by quoting scripture from Psalms 91:11-12 (NLT). Satan was trying to get Jesus to demonstrate his powers to draw attention unto himself and test his Faith in God's Word that promised to save Him. Again, Jesus quotes from the Word of God (Deuteronomy 6:16 NASB), "It is also written: 'Do not put the Lord your God to the test.'"

- This temptation is the Pride of Life. The Pride of Life can be defined as anything that is "of the world," meaning anything that leads to arrogance, ostentation, pride in self, presumption, and boasting. It is also seen in the stubborn mind-set that will not allow an individual to repent of or confess their sins.

The Third Temptation:

- Verses 8 and 9 state, Again, the devil took him to a very high mountain and showed him all the kingdoms of the world and their splendor. "All this I will give you," he said, "if you will bow down and worship me." Jesus then quotes from Deuteronomy 6:13 (KJV) to Satan, "Away from me, Satan! For it is written: 'Worship the Lord your God, and serve him only.'" This Temptation is called the Lust of the Eye. The Lust of the Eyes is best described as eyes lured by and delighted with riches and the material things of this world; this lust is also called covetousness. Satan shows us his power of influence; He tempts us with wealth, splendor, and earthly glory spread out before us on TV, billboards, movies, magazines, etc., which are never eternal.

- The devil wants us to worship him to achieve position, power, money, and/or status in this life. Christians must never bow down to anything or anyone except the Lord our God. Luke tells us: "For what does it profit a man if he gains the whole world and loses or forfeits himself" (Luke 9:25 ESV)?

When we look at these temptations, we see they are the same temptations Adam and Eve were tempted with. We see the temptation of the Lust of the Flesh, the Lust of the Eye, and the biggest sin – the Pride of Life. Which is also the three "P's" – Pleasure, Popularity and Power.

> The Bible tells us, . . . The woman saw that the fruit of the tree was good for food (Trick #1 Lust of the flesh) and pleasing to the eyes (Trick #2 Lust of the eye) and also desirable for gaining wisdom (Trick #3 The Pride of life) (Genesis 3:6 ESV).

Note: Every sin that mankind commits are from this bag of tricks or temptations in which Adam and Eve fell from.

Jesus was offered the same temptation as Adam and Eve, but He answered with a very different response! Jesus demonstrated for us how to say NO to the world and YES to the Word of God. Satan will always promise or offer us the world; but in the end his way is the way to death and eternal separation from God/Jesus.

In the book of Luke, Jesus gives us a parable called the Rich Fool. In this parable Jesus teaches us that the world, and the things in it, will last only for a little while and that our hearts should never be about material earthly things. These are the types of things that are foolish in God's eyes.

The Rich Fool

"And He told them a parable, saying, "The land of a rich man was very productive. And he began thinking to himself, saying, 'What shall I do, since I have no place to store my crops?' And he said, 'This is what I will do: I will tear down my barns and build larger ones, and I will store all my grain and my goods there. And I will say to myself, "You have many goods stored up for many years to come; relax, eat, drink, and enjoy yourself!"' But God said to him, 'You fool! This very night your soul is demanded of you; and as for all that you have prepared, who will own it now?' Such is the one who stores up treasure for himself, and is not rich in relation to God" (Luke 12:16-21 NASB).

Again, the Bible asks: "For what does it profit a man to gain the whole world and forfeit his soul" (Mark 8:36 ESV)?

In the book of John Chapter Seventeen Jesus said that we are not of the world, but that He has sent us into the world for His purpose and His will.

"I have given them Your word; and the world has hated them because they are not of the world, just as I am not of the world. I do not pray that You should take them out of the world, but that You should keep them from the evil one. They are not of the world, just as I am not of the world. Sanctify them by Your truth. Your word is truth. As You sent Me into the world, I also have sent them into the world. And for their sakes I sanctify Myself, that they also may be sanctified by the truth" (John 17:14-19 NKJV).

In verses 17 and 19 Jesus uses the word "sanctify" as the idea of setting apart for a holy purpose. Here He sanctifies all believers unto Himself that we may be set apart for the Father's will by the truth He brought us.

Jesus teaches us that it's the Word of God that is the key to overcoming this world. He made statements like:

- "Truly, truly, I say to you, the one who hears My word, and believes Him who sent Me, has eternal life, and does not come into judgment, but has passed out of death into life" (John 5:24 NASB).

- "I tell you the truth, anyone who obeys my teaching will never die" (John 8:51 NLT)!

- "So Jesus saying to those Jews who had believed Him, "If you continue in My word, then you are truly My disciples. And you shall know the truth, and the truth shall make you free" (John 8:31-32 NASB).

The first thing Jesus says to us is to believe in Him. Our first step in this pursuit is our faith/belief that Jesus is the Christ, Messiah and the Son of God.

The second step is an obedience and dedication to the Word of God. Jesus tells us to continue in His word. The word "continue" means to have a habit of abiding, to maintain, or to position oneself in the Word. This means that anyone that continues in the teaching of Jesus Christ would find salvation and truth, liberating them from this sinful world. These two steps are how we say NO to the world and YES to the Word of God.

Let's look at the Apostle Paul. One of the first things we know about Paul is that the Bible calls him a servant of Christ Jesus, a called apostle and set apart (separated) for the gospel of God (Romans 1:1, Galatians 1:15, and Acts 13:2 BSB). Here is what Paul has to say about separation from this world:

"And do not be conformed to this world, but be transformed by the renewing of your mind, that you may prove what is that good and acceptable and perfect will of God" (Romans 12:2 NKJV).

First, Paul tells us to stop living like the world (value system or lifestyle), and be transformed by the renewing of our minds. The word transformed comes from the Greek word "metamorphoo," meaning "metamorphosis"– change from the inside out. He also said, then we change from the inside out, we can test and approve what God's will is—His good, pleasing and perfect will.

Note: God has ONLY ONE will and it is good, pleasing and perfect.

Paul tells the church at Colossae and us how to live Holy lives in order to surpass the righteousness of the Pharisees and the teachers of the law. He says:

> "Therefore, since you have been raised with Christ, strive for the things above, where Christ is seated at the right hand of God. Set your minds on things above, not on earthly things. For you died, and your life is now hidden with Christ in God. When Christ, who is your life, appears, then you also will appear with Him in glory. Put to death, therefore, the components of your earthly nature: sexual immorality, impurity, lust, evil desires, and greed, which is idolatry. Because of these, the wrath of God is coming on the sons of disobedience. When you lived among them, you also used to walk in these ways. But now you must put aside all such things as these: anger, rage, malice, slander, and filthy language from your lips. Do not lie to one another, since you have taken off the old self with its practices, and have put on the new self, which is being renewed in knowledge in the image of its Creator (Colossians 3:1-10 BSB)."

Paul understood that our greatest battles would take place in our minds, and he also knew that the un-renewed mind would be a playground for Satan. Paul and the other apostles understood there is a need for us to renew our minds. The Apostle James said it this way – a double-minded man is unstable in all he does.

In one of Paul's letters he wrote to the church in Corinth, he reminded them they were no longer worldly, but that they were spiritual. He told them there would be people in this world who think that Christians are to live by the standards of this world. However, Paul told them that Christians are not of this world and that Christians don't war or fight as the world.

> "I beg of you that when I am present I may not have to show boldness with such confidence as I count on showing against some who suspect us of walking according to the flesh. For though we walk in the flesh, we are not waging war according to the flesh. For the weapons of our warfare are not of the flesh but have divine power to destroy strongholds. We destroy arguments and every lofty opinion raised against the knowledge of God, and take every thought captive to obey Christ" (2 Corinthians 10:2-5 ESV).

The Apostle James informs us in his forth chapter, that if anyone want to be a friend of the world; we are enemies of God. And James calls these individuals adulterers. He said, "You adulterous people, don't you know that friendship with the world means enmity against God? Therefore, anyone who chooses to be a friend of the world becomes an enemy of God" (James 4:4 NIV).

Now that we are to be separate from this world we live in (in everything that we do) how does God expect us to accomplish this? This is not an easy thing for anyone to do in the natural, but there is nothing that is impossible with God (Jeremiah 32:17, 27; Luke 1:37 KJV).

The key to a renewed mind and transformed life is through the Word of God. Matthew 4:1-11, Luke 4:1-12 and Mark 1:12-13 describe the temptations of Jesus; He demonstrated for us how to overcome the world's temptations and Satan; it was and it is through the "Word of God." This is done by reading it, praying it, meditating it, and reflecting on it. By doing these things through the power of the Holy Spirit, we begin to have the mind of Christ. Paul states, "Let this mind (attitude) be in you which was also in Christ Jesus" (Philippians 2:5 NKJV).

First by the hearing of God's Word:

- "So then faith comes by hearing, and hearing by the word of God" (Romans 10:17 NKJV).

- "Let the word of Christ richly dwell within you as you teach and admonish one another with all wisdom, and as you sing psalms, hymns, and spiritual songs with gratitude in your hearts to God" (Colossians 3:16 BSB).

Second, by spending time in the Word of God:

- "You shall teach them to your children, talking of them when you are sitting in your house, and when you are walking by the way, and when you lie down, and when you rise. You shall write them on the doorposts of your house and on your gates, that your days and the days of your children may be multiplied in the land that the LORD swore to your fathers to give them, as long as the heavens are above the earth (Deuteronomy 11:19-21 ESV).

- "So they read from the Book of the Law of God, explaining it and giving insight, so that the people could understand what was being read" (Nehemiah 8:8 BSB).

Third, by devoting ourselves to God's Word:

- Paul tells Timothy, "Be diligent to present yourself approved to God as a worker who does not need to be ashamed, accurately handling the word of truth" (2 Timothy 2:15 NASB).

- "Until I come, devote yourself to the public reading of Scripture, to preaching and to teaching" (1 Timothy 4:13 NIV).

Fourth by meditating on the Word of God:

- "This Book of the Law shall not depart from your mouth, but you shall meditate in it day and night, that you may observe to do according to all that is written in it. ". ". . . For then you will make your way prosperous, and then you will have good success" (Joshua 1:8 NKJV).

- "But his delight is in the law of the LORD, And in His law he meditates day and night" (Psalm 1:2 NKJV).

- "Be angry, and do not sin. Meditate within your heart on your bed, and be still. Selah" (Psalm 4:4 NKJV)

Fifth by, memorizing the Word of God:

- "Your word I have hidden in my heart, That I might not sin against You" (Psalms 119:11 NKJV).

- "But the word is very near you, in your mouth and in your heart, that you may do it" (Deuteronomy 30:14 NKJV).

Sixth by, praying using the Word of God:

- Jesus said referring to prayer; "If you remain in me and my words remain in you, ask whatever you wish, and it will be given you" (John 15:7 NIV).

- James said, "Now if any of you lacks wisdom, he should ask God, who gives generously to all without finding fault, and it will be given to him" (James 1:5 BSB).

- Paul states, "Finally brothers, pray for us, that the word of the Lord may spread quickly and be held in honor, just as it was with you" (2 Thessalonians 3:1 BSB).

We are to live in this world, but be separate from this world. This can't be done by our own power or strength, but it can be achieved through the Holy Spirit and Jesus Christ our Lord and Savior dwelling and working inside of us. The Bible tells us: "Not by might nor by power, but by My Spirit,' Says the LORD of hosts" (Zechariah 4:6 NKJV).

PRAYER:

Dear Jesus, please help me to live in this world as you did . . . by the Word of God and the power of the Holy Spirit. Father God lead me and guide my actions and reaction, that all that I say and do may bring you glory. In Jesus' name – AMEN

Reflection Time:

1. How can a Christian be in this world, and not be a part of this world?

   _____

   _____

   _____

   _____

   _____

   _____

   _____

   _____

   _____

   _____

2. How does a person come out from under this world's system and live separate?

   _____

   _____

   _____

   _____

   _____

   _____

   _____

3. What things might you have that may be a worldly stronghold? And why?

   _____

   _____

   _____

   _____

   _____

   _____

   _____

4. What step will you commit to take to separate yourself from this world?

_____

_____

_____

_____

_____

_____

_____

5. How much time are you spending in the Word of God? What's stopping you from spending more time in His Word?

_____

_____

_____

_____

_____

_____

_____

_____

6. Who will be the person that will hold you accountable in this area?

_____

_____

_____

_____

_____

_____

7. How can you apply what you've learned in this chapter to your personal life?

_____

_____

_____

_____

_____

_____

_____

_____

_____

_____

"For what does it profit a man if he gains the whole world and loses or forfeits himself (Luke 9:25 ESV)?

"The more your heart turns to Jesus, the more your heart will turn away from the world!"

Chapter Five

"Understanding Who I Really Am"

"How does God see you?"

"You are the salt of the earth; but if the salt has become tasteless, how can it be made salty again? It is no longer good for anything, except to be thrown out and trampled underfoot by people. "You are the light of the world. A city set on a hill cannot be hidden; nor do people light a lamp and put it under a basket, but on the lampstand, and it gives light to all who are in the house. Your light must shine before people in such a way that they may see your good works, and glorify your Father who is in heaven" (Matthew 5:13-16 NASB).

I love watching movies; one of my all-time favorites is Avatar. The reason I like it so much is because the characters who were connected often said to one another, "I see you," meaning they could see the true spirit inside the other. They could see through the outward appearance and truthfully say, "I see you!"

Unfortunately, this is not true with us. We all wear a mask at some time or another. Sometimes we wear them so much and we have worn them for so long we don't even know ourselves.

In Matthew Chapter Five Jesus points out "Who" and "What" we are. He calls believers Salt and Light to illustrate the impact Christians would make in this world. This impact brings glory and honor to God.

I've heard that we all should have three strong relationships: one with God, one with others, and one with ourselves. This chapter is designed around the third relationship, the relationship with yourself, the person God created.

Do you know who you are? Can you honestly answer these four simple questions?[10]

- What did God create me to be?
- What are the gifts and talents God given me?
- What is my God-given ministry?
- What are my strengths and weaknesses?

In this chapter I'll discuss more about the impact that Christians make in the world. Jesus uses two simple things (Salt and Light) to illustrate who we are, what we are here for, and what we should be doing as His disciples.

First Salt:

- Salt creates a thirst; it seasons; it preserves. Salt maintains its essence, its true character.

The second is Light:

- Light illuminates and gives direction. As light, Christians are to give godly direction and to positively influence to others. So people will see you are different as you grow in the Lord, and they will desire to discover what makes you different.

Salt and Light are descriptive of who we are. The most important thing we should know about ourselves is that no one can give us an accurate view of ourselves; ONLY GOD can! He is the one that created us and made us what He wanted us to be and it's all for His glory.

- "This is the book of the generations of Adam. In the day that God created man, in the likeness of God made he him; Male and female created he them; and blessed them, and called their name Adam, in the day when they were created" (Genesis 5:1-2 KJV).

- "Did not he that made me in the womb make him? and did not one fashion us in the womb" (Job 31:15 KJV)?

- "Your hands have made me and fashioned me; Give me understanding, that I may learn Your commandments" (Psalms 119:73 NKJV).

- "Everyone who is called by my name, whom I created for my glory, whom I formed and made" (Isaiah 43:7 NIV).

- "Before I formed you in the womb I knew you, and before you were born I consecrated you; I appointed you a prophet to the nations" (Jeremiah 1:5 ESV).

- "For we are God's masterpiece. He has created us anew in Christ Jesus, so we can do the good things he planned for us long ago" (Ephesians 2:10 NLT).

It's sad that most Christians have a wrong idea of God's opinion of themselves. We usually base our opinions on the way we've been taught, the way we make assumptions, and the way we interpret our experiences. Our processing differs greatly from God's Some Christians believe that God is disappointed in them and that they'll never measure up. Some may even think that God is angry with them. This being said, if we want a healthy identity, we must first understand the truth about ourselves. In other words, God's opinion of us is the foundation for a healthy identity.

In the book of Matthew Jesus said, "For whoever exalts himself will be humbled, and whoever humbles himself will be exalted" (Matthew 23:12 BSB). Here Jesus teaches us that we don't need to puff ourselves up or try to impress anyone. The Bible tells us we are "fearfully and wonderfully made" (Psalm 139:14 KJV). So that means that God doesn't make junk, and every one of us is His unique masterpiece. As His creation and a child of God we must realize that He has created billions of individuals and yet He has given each of us our own look, our own strengths, our own personality, and our own potential. We are perfect in the eyes of God, and He made us just the way He wanted us!

In the Bible, we have two instances where Jesus received affirmation of who He was from the Father; at His Baptism and again on the Mountain of Transfiguration.

The Baptism of Jesus

"Then Jesus came from Galilee to the Jordan to John, to be baptized by him. John would have prevented him, saying, "I need to be baptized by you, and do you come to me?" But Jesus answered him, "Let it be so now, for thus it is fitting for us to fulfill all righteousness." Then he consented. And when Jesus was baptized, immediately he went up from the water, and behold, the heavens were opened to him, and he saw the Spirit of God descending like a dove and coming to rest on him; and behold, a voice from heaven said, "This is my beloved Son, with whom I am well pleased" (Matthew 3:13-17 ESV).

The Transfiguration of Jesus

"And after six days Jesus took with him Peter and James, and John his brother, and led them up a high mountain by themselves. And he was transfigured before them, and his face shone like the sun, and his clothes became white as light. And behold, there appeared to them Moses and Elijah, talking with him. And Peter said to Jesus, "Lord, it is good that we are here. If you wish, I will make three tents here, one for you and one for Moses and one for Elijah." He was still speaking when, behold, a bright cloud overshadowed them, and a voice from the cloud said, "This is my beloved Son, with whom I am well pleased; listen to him" (Matthew 17:1-5 ESV)!

Here we find God telling the world who Jesus is: "This is my Son, whom I love; with him I am well pleased. Listen to him." And every one of us needs someone else to tell us who we are, and it is in the Word of God. God has told us throughout the Bible who we are in his eyes also.

However, the world is persistent in its trying to tell us who we are and what we need to do (where we should work, live and go to school); how we should look (cosmetic surgery, hair coloring, hair extensions, and colored contact lenses); how we should act; and what we should wear. But the Word of God tells us we are perfect in the eyes of God, and He made us just the way He wanted us.

When we learn to see ourselves as God sees us, we will begin to experience true happiness in our lives, and we will stop depending on this world for approval. This will be the day when your regeneration, justification, sanctification and glorification will take on a brand-new life of its own. Understand, God has said to all of us; this is my son; this is my daughter whom I love; and He is well pleased with His children; God has called us His very own.

Now let's look at the Apostle Paul and see what he has to say to us about understanding who we are. Paul states:

> "For by the grace given me I say to every one of you: Do not think of yourself more highly than you ought, but think of yourself with sober judgment, according to the measure of faith God has given you" (Romans 12:3 BSB).

Here Paul is talking about how we should think about ourselves. He said, we should think soberly, the opposite of being drunk. We shouldn't walk around like a drunken person, not having a clear understanding about ourselves. We should all ask ourselves one question: Do I see myself as God sees me, or do I see myself through the eyes of the world?

We all should understand that the world only sees from the outside, but God the Father sees the real you. A person can be the most beautiful person in the world on the outside but have a heart full of darkness and sin in the eyes of the Jesus Christ. So, this is why Paul says we should have a clear view of ourselves.

Once we see ourselves through the eyes of God/Jesus; it is then we will understand that we have received approval and favor from God the Father, we have been equipped, and we will be held responsible and accountable for the things He has entrusted us with. Jesus says: "From everyone who has been given much, much will be required; and from him who has been entrusted with much, even more will be demanded" (Luke 12:48 BSB).[11]

First, Jesus tells us we are approved and favored:

- "For he chose us in him before the creation of the world to be holy and blameless in his sight. In love" (Ephesians 1:4 NIV).

- "Then he said, 'The God of our fathers has chosen you that you should know His will, and see the Just One, and hear the voice of His mouth" (Acts 22:14 NKJV).

- "But you are a chosen generation, a royal priesthood, a holy nation, His own special people, that you may proclaim the praises of Him who called you out of darkness into His marvelous light" (1 Peter 2:9 NKJV)

- "I no longer call you servants, because a servant does not know his master's business. Instead, I have called you friends, for everything that I learned from my Father I have made known to you. You did not choose me, but I chose you and appointed you so that you might go and bear fruit—fruit that will last—and so that whatever you ask in my name the Father will give you" (John 15:15-16 NIV).

Here again, we find that Jesus wants that relationship with us. In these verses above we are chosen and are called friend. God calls us friend; that's right the Bible calls us a Friend of God!

Second, the Bible tells us we have been equipped:

- "Each of you should use whatever gift you have received to serve others, as faithful stewards of God's grace in its various forms" (1 Peter 4:10 NIV).

- "For the gifts and the calling of God are irrevocable" (Romans 11:29 ESV). *Irrevocable means: not able to be revoked, changed, or undone.*

- "For as we have many members in one body, but all the members do not have the same function, so we, being many, are one body in Christ, and individually members of one another. Having then gifts differing according to the grace that is given to us, let us use them: if prophecy, let us prophesy in proportion to our faith; or ministry, let us use it in our ministering; he who teaches, in teaching; he who exhorts, in exhortation; he who gives, with liberality; he who leads, with diligence; he who shows mercy, with cheerfulness" (Romans 12:4-8 NKJV).

- "Now may the God of peace, who brought up from the dead the great Shepherd of the sheep through the blood of the eternal covenant, that is, Jesus our Lord, equip you in every good thing to do His will, working in us that which is pleasing in His sight, through Jesus Christ, to whom be the glory forever and ever. Amen" (Hebrews 13:20-21 NASB).

We all have the ability to be who God says we are and the ability to do what He has commanded.

First, it's God who has gifted us all and He has deposited His Spirit into every believer.

Secondly, we don't get to choose our abilities or our gifts; it's the Holy Spirit that determines our gifts. It's our responsibility to find out what our gift or gifts are and develop them.

Our abilities and gifts are given to us for two very important reasons: for the glory of God and to serve one another. So this means that as Christians we are equipped to do whatever we are called by God to do.

Third, the Bible also tells us we are all accountable:

- "For God will bring every deed into judgment, including every hidden thing, whether it is good or evil" (Ecclesiastes 12:14 NIV).

- "... For we will all stand before the judgment seat of God; for it is written, "As I live, says the Lord, every knee shall bow to me, and every tongue shall confess to God." So then each of us will give an account of himself to God (Romans 14:10-12 ESV).

- God "will repay each one according to his deeds" (Romans 2:6 BSB).

- "Because you know that the Lord will reward each one for whatever good they do, whether they are slave or free" (Ephesians 6:8 NIV).

- "For we must all appear before the judgment seat of Christ, that each one may receive his due for the things done in the body, whether good or bad" (2 Corinthians 5:10 BSB).

The Bible tells us in the Old and New Testaments that one day we all will stand before the judgment seat of Jesus Christ and that we'll all give an account of our deeds.

For the non-Christian, it will be a judgment for rejecting Jesus as their Lord and Savior and for the sinful acts committed throughout their lives.

Christians, on the other hand, will be judged for our stewardship. We will all stand before Jesus and give an account of the time, energy, gifts, talents, and opportunity He has deposited in each of us. The Apostle John tells us that Jesus has called us to bear fruit that will last. The Bible states:

> "Now if anyone builds on this foundation with gold, silver, precious stones, wood, hay, straw, each one's work will become clear; for the Day will declare it, because it will be revealed by fire; and the fire will test each one's work, of what sort it is. If anyone's work which he has

built on it endures, he will receive a reward. If anyone's work is burned, he will suffer loss; but he himself will be saved, yet so as through fire" (1 Corinthians 3:12-15 NKJV).

"You did not choose me, but I chose you and appointed you that you should go and bear fruit and that your fruit should abide, so that whatever you ask the Father in my name, he may give it to you" (John 15:16 ESV).

Understand, through the eyes of Jesus we have received approval and favor from God the Father, we are gifted and equipped to do great works, and we are held accountable for all of our actions.

However, if we want to know the truth about who we are, we must go to the source, God Himself. God tells us how He sees us and how we should view ourselves throughout His Word (the Bible). What we learn from His Word will help us in our relationship with God, with others, and ourselves.

Our heavenly Father loves us and sees us as He sees Christ Jesus. As Christians, we are not orphans or strangers to God. Before He formed us in our mother's womb, He knew us. God knew us before we were even born. He has set every one of us apart for Himself and appointed each of us a particular task designed with each individual in mind (Jeremiah 1:5 NLT).

In the book of Judges, the Angel of the Lord appeared to Gideon and called him "A Mighty Man of Valor" (Judges 6:12 KJV)! However, everyone, including Gideon himself, believed Gideon to be a coward. It was unlikely that anyone would consider him a hero. But God picked Gideon to lead Israel in revolt against the Midianites. The thing to take note of isn't that God picked Gideon, but it's how God saw Gideon. When God looked at Gideon, He didn't see a wheat thresher or a timid coward. God saw Gideon as a Mighty Man of Valor! According to Webster's dictionary, the word "valor" means strength of mind or spirit that enables a man to encounter danger with firmness; personal bravery; heroism. Regardless of how other people see us, God sees what He's created us to be and how we are best used for His glory.

We find our identity in the Word of God. It's there where we read and begin to understand how we owe it all to Jesus. His life, death, burial, and resurrection are key in establishing our relationship with God because our new Christian identity is in Him! So as we go through the Bible, we can almost hear the voice of God/Jesus telling us "who" and "what" we are in His eyes and we can confidently say to ourselves:

- I AM – God's child, I born again, not of corruptible seed, but of incorruptible, by the Word of God (1 Peter 1:23 KJV).

- I AM – Forgiven of all my sins (Ephesians 1:7 KJV) and the blood of Jesus, his Son, cleanses us from all sin (1 John 1:7 NLT)

- I AM – A New Creature (2 Corinthians 5:17 NASB)

- I AM – The Temple of the Holy Spirit (1 Corinthians 6:19 KJV)

- I AM – Delivered from the power of darkness and translated into God's kingdom (Colossians 1:13 KJV).

- I AM – Redeemed from the curse of the law (Galatians 3:13 NASB).

- I AM – A Saint (Romans 1:7 KJV; Philippians 1:1 NKJV).

- I AM – Blessed (Deuteronomy 28:2-14 ESV; Galatians 3:9 KJV).

- I AM – The Head and not the tail (Deuteronomy 28:13 NKJV).

- I AM – Holy and without blame before Him in love (Ephesians 1:4 KJV).

- I AM – Victorious (Revelation 21:7 NLT).

- I AM – Set Free (John 8:32-33 NLT).

- I AM – Strong in the Lord and in His mighty power (Ephesians 6:10 NLT).

- I AM – Dead to sin (Romans 6:2, 11 BLB)

- I AM – More than a conqueror through him that loved us (Romans 8:37 KJV).

- I AM – Joint heir with Christ (Romans 8:17 NKJV).

- I AM – Complete in Him (Colossians 2:10 KJV).

- I AM – Crucified with Christ (Galatians 2:20 ESV).

- I AM – Alive together with Christ (Ephesians 2:5 ESV).

- I AM – Reconciled to God (2 Corinthians 5:18 KJV).

- I AM – Free from Condemnation (Romans 8:1 KJV).

- I AM – Firmly rooted, built up, established in the faith (Colossians 2:7 NASB).

- I AM – Born of God; and the evil one does not touch me (1 John 5:18 NKJV).

- I AM – The Righteousness of God (2 Corinthians 5:21 ESV; 1 Peter 2:24 NKJV).

- I AM – Chosen (1 Thessalonians 1:4 BSB; Ephesians 1:4 BSB; 1 Peter 2:9 BSB).

- I AM – The Apple of My Father's Eye (Deuteronomy 32:10 KJV; Psalm 17:8 KJV).

- I AM – Healed by the stripes of Jesus (1 Peter 2:24 NKJV; Isaiah 53:5 NKJV).

- I AM – Being changed and transformed into His image (2 Corinthians 3:18 NKJV).

- I AM – Raised up with Christ and seated in heavenly places (Ephesians 2:6 NASB).

- I AM – Beloved of God (Romans 1:7 NKJV; 1 Thessalonians 1:4 KJV).

- I AM – The light of the world (Matthew 5:14 BLB).

- I AM – Built up in Him and established in the faith (Colossians 2:7 NKJV).

- I AM – One in Christ (John 17:22 NLT).

As we close this chapter, there are four important things we should understand better about ourselves:

- Our right standing with God is through the righteousness that comes from Jesus Christ our Lord, and the indwelling of the Holy Spirit.

- Our identity and purpose comes from God.

- We are His masterpiece.

- He made us to love Him and to reflect who He is.

Now the question is, how do you see yourself? In the book of Numbers, the Bible tells us that the children of Israel failed to go into the Promised Land. When we read the account in Numbers 13:33 (NKJV), we find the words, "And we were like grasshoppers in our own sight, and so we were in their sight." The reason the Israelites were so afraid to fight the people of Canaan wasn't because the Canaanites were giants, but, because the Israelites saw themselves so small! It was how the Israelites viewed themselves that defeated them. Therefore, as believers, if we don't choose to see ourselves as conquering children of God, the devil will keep us from becoming the people God has called us to be. When we see ourselves as God sees us, it will change our entire outlook on life. Living life knowing that we are children of God and that He loves us is a wonderful and blessed life for anyone to live. Knowing who we are in Christ Jesus is not a life of arrogance, self-righteousness, or pride, but a life of fulfillment.

PRAYER:

Father God, I thank you for my life, health, and strength. Father I pray that you would make me ... shape me ... and create within me the likeness of your Son Jesus Christ. Help me to take hold of the masterpiece you have made within me. And please Holy Spirit help me keep my mind on the fact that my identity and purpose come from God alone. In Jesus' name – AMEN

Reflection Time:

1. Do you know who you are? Honestly answer these four simple questions?

    _____

    _____

    _____

    _____

    a. What did God make me to be?

    _____

    _____

    _____

    _____

    b. What are my gifts and talents?

    _____

    _____

    _____

    _____

    c. What is my ministry unto God?

    _____

    _____

    _____

    _____

    d. What are my strengths and weaknesses?

    _____

    _____

    _____

    _____

2. Before reading this chapter, what was your view of yourself? And why?

    _____

    _____

    _____

_____
_____
_____

3. What are the four important things you should understand better about yourself?

   • One:

   _____
   _____
   _____

   • Two:

   _____
   _____
   _____

   • Three:

   _____
   _____
   _____

   • Four:

   _____
   _____
   _____

4. Tell of a time when you struggled with self-esteem?

   _____
   _____
   _____
   _____
   _____
   _____
   _____

5. What step will you commit to take in order to maintain the Christian self-image of yourself?

_____

_____

_____

_____

_____

_____

_____

_____

6. Who will be the person that will hold you accountable in this area?

_____

_____

_____

_____

_____

_____

_____

_____

7. The Bible tells us we are "_____" (Psalm 139:14).

8. Ask yourself, do I see myself as God sees me, or do I see myself through the eyes of the world? Explain your answer.

_____

_____

_____

_____

_____

_____

_____

_____

9. How can you apply what you've learned in this chapter to your personal life?

_____

_____

_____

_____

_____

_____

_____

_____

_____

_____

"So, remember that we are what the Word of God says we are!"

"Understanding who I really am is to understand who God sees when He looks at me."

"Take the mask off and love the real you, the person God made you to be!"

Chapter Six

"Christian Community"

"Serving the Body of Christ"

"If you love those who love you, what reward will you get? Are not even the tax collectors doing that? And if you greet only your own people, what are you doing more than others? Do not even pagans do that? Be perfect, therefore, as your heavenly Father is perfect" (Matthew 5:46-48 NIV).

Most churches I know have their own little cliques, their groups of upper, middle, and lower-class members in it. I would say that in most of our churches today, there are members of the church that leave Sunday morning worship service each Sunday and do not feel like they are a part of the church. I would even dare say that all of us at one time or another have felt that way.

I tell you that most churches do not know or understand what true Christian Community is all about. Most believers today think that Christian Community is Sunday morning worship service and midweek Bible study, but it's much more than just coming to church.

In Chapter One, we talked about our relationship with God/Jesus as the most important relationship anyone could have. And in the last chapter, we talked about the relationship we should have with ourselves. In this chapter we'll spend time talking about another relationship, our relationship with other people. God/Jesus wants all Christians to understand that genuine Christian community is at the center, and it's the foundation of our Christianity. Jesus stated:

> "A new commandment I give to you, that you love one another; as I have loved you, that you also love one another. By this all will know that you are My disciples, if you have love for one another" (John 13:34-35 NKJV).

These words are some of the last teachings that Jesus gave His disciples before going to the cross. As we look at the verses, we understand that Jesus is giving us a command, and not just a suggestion to have genuine Christian community. He knew that the gospel would be validated by the profound love that Christians have for one another.

This Christian community could be seen in the fellowship of the believers in the early Church in the book of Acts:

> "They devoted themselves to the apostles' teaching and to the fellowship, to the breaking of bread and to prayer. A sense of awe came over everyone, and the apostles performed many wonders and signs. All the believers were together and had everything in common. Selling their possessions and goods, they shared with anyone who was in need. With one accord they continued to meet daily in the temple courts and to break bread from house to house, sharing their meals with gladness and sincerity of heart, praising God and enjoying the favor of all the people. And the Lord added to their number daily those who were being saved" (Acts 2:42-47 BSB).

- First – We find that the early Church spent time in the Word of God. Verse 42 said they devoted themselves to it.

- Second – They spent time fellowshipping (v 42 and 46), and they broke bread and had prayer together.

- Third – They held everything in common giving to anyone in need (v 44 and 45).

Jesus always modeled the way Christians should behave by His actions. He never told people to do anything He did not do. The Bible tells us how He demonstrated genuine Christian community His entire life through His acts of service and love. Just look at the Last Supper, the Bible tells us:

The Passover Meal and Last Supper

"It was now just before the Passover Feast, and Jesus knew that His hour had come to leave this world and return to the Father. Having loved His own who were in the world, He loved them to the very end. The evening meal was underway, and the devil had already put into the heart of Judas, the son of Simon Iscariot, to betray Jesus. Jesus knew that the Father had delivered all things into His hands, and that He had come from God and was returning to God. So He got up from the supper, laid aside His outer garments, and wrapped a towel around His waist. After that, He poured water into a basin and began to wash the disciples' feet and dry them with the towel that was around Him" (John 13:1-5 BSB).

"When Jesus had washed their feet and put on His outer garments, He reclined with them again and asked, "Do you know what I have done for you? You call Me Teacher and Lord, and rightly so, because I am. So if I, your Lord and Teacher, have washed your feet, you also should wash one another's feet. I have set you an example so that you should do as I have done for you. Truly, truly, I tell you, no servant is greater than his master, nor is a messenger greater than the one who sent him. If you know these things; you will be blessed if you do them" (John 13:12-17 BSB).

Let's look closely at what happened the night of the Passover meal and how Jesus demonstrates genuine Christian community.[12]

- It was a planned event (v1)

- It took place over a meal (v2)

- They received the Word of God (v2)

- Genuine Christian service of love was shone (4-5)

- They received eternal teaching (v12-16)

Here Jesus demonstrated to us by His acts in this passage what Christian community and its self-sacrificing love looked like. This kind of love is not defined by our feelings, but by our acts of love through our service.

Throughout the gospels (Matthew, Mark, Luke, John) we find Jesus serving everywhere He went; it was His lifestyle. In Matthew chapter twenty-five, Jesus tells us that at His second coming, He's coming to judge, and at this judgment He will separate the unbelievers and the pretenders from the true believers. Here He will judge us from the command He gave to us to Love one another, as He have loved us. We find this truth in Matthew twenty-five in the parable of the sheep and the goats.

The Sheep and the Goats

"When the Son of Man comes in his glory, and all the angels with him, he will sit on his glorious throne. All the nations will be gathered before him, and he will separate the people one from another as a shepherd separates the sheep from the goats. He will put the sheep on his right and the goats on his left. "Then the King will say to those on his right, 'Come, you who are blessed by my Father; take your inheritance, the kingdom prepared for you since the creation of the world. For I was hungry and you gave me something to eat, I was thirsty and you gave me something to drink, I was a stranger and you invited me in, I needed clothes and you clothed me, I was sick and you looked after me, I was in prison and you came to visit me.' "Then the righteous will answer him, 'Lord, when did we see you hungry and feed you, or thirsty and give you something to drink? When did we see you a stranger and invite you in, or needing clothes and clothe you? When did we see you sick or in prison and go to visit you?' "The King will reply, 'Truly I tell you, whatever you did for one of the least of these brothers and sisters of mine, you did for me.' "Then he will say to those on his left, 'Depart from me, you who are cursed, into the eternal fire prepared for the devil and his angels. For I was hungry and you gave me nothing to eat, I was thirsty and you gave me nothing to drink, I was a stranger and you did not invite me in, I needed clothes and you did not clothe me, I was sick and in prison and you did not look after me.' "They also will answer, 'Lord, when did we see you hungry or thirsty or a stranger or needing clothes or sick or in prison, and did not help you?' "He will reply, 'Truly I tell you, whatever you did not do for one of the least of these, you did not do for me.' "Then they will go away to eternal punishment, but the righteous to eternal life" (Matthew 25:31-46 NIV).

To treat everyone we come into contact with like they are Jesus is not easy; this is why we need the help of the Holy Spirit in our lives. We must understand that the way we treat other people demonstrates our obedience and love to God/Jesus.

In the Book of Matthew, we learn of an occasion where a person who was an expert in the religious law (a lawyer) tried to test Jesus (Matthew 22:35 NLT). He asked Jesus, what must I do to inherit eternal life? Jesus replied by saying, what does the Law say? The expert answered: Love the Lord your God with all your heart and with all your soul and with all your strength and with all your mind; and, Love your neighbor as yourself; quoting Deuteronomy 6:5 and Leviticus 19:18 (KJV). Jesus told the expert he had given the correct answer. Then He said to him that if he loved God and his neighbor, he would inherit eternal life. However, the Bible tells us that the man wanted to justify himself by asking Jesus, "who is my neighbor?" Jesus responded with the parable of the Good Samaritan.

The Good Samaritan

"Jesus replied, "A man was going down from Jerusalem to Jericho, and he fell among robbers, who stripped him and beat him and departed, leaving him half dead. Now by chance a priest was going down that road, and when he saw him he passed by on the other side. So likewise a Levite, when he came to the place and saw him, passed by on the other side. But a Samaritan, as he journeyed, came to where he was, and when he saw him, he had compassion. He went to him and bound up his wounds, pouring on oil and wine. Then he set him on his own animal and brought him to an inn and took care of him. And the next day he took out two denarii and gave them to the innkeeper, saying, 'Take care of him, and whatever more you spend, I will repay you when I come back.' Which of these three, do you think, proved to be a neighbor to the man who fell among the robbers?" He said, "The one who showed him mercy." And Jesus said to him, "You go, and do likewise" (Luke 10:30-37 ESV).

This Parable, the Good Samaritan, is one of the greatest illustrations of true human kindness. This parable is not only a call to help those we see in need, it's also a warning against self-centered action, legalistic religion and uncompassionated service.

Again, the standard for a genuine Christian community is to love; loving God and loving our neighbor as ourselves. The two Greek words for love are Agape and Phileo.

- Agape or Agapao means: the highest form of love. Agape is considered to be the love originating from God or Christ for mankind and is completely selfless and totally committed.

- Phileo means: This love is companionable and relational. It's a brotherly/ friendship love.

- Note: In the opening verses of this chapter, I used Matthew 5:46-48 (NIV). In verse 48 tells us to, "Be perfect, therefore, as your heavenly Father is perfect." The Greek word for perfect here is teleios which refers to maturity and completeness. Jesus expects us to relate to one another in God's love (Agape) as the Father relates to us. Only then will we be perfect.

The Apostle James tells us, "If you really fulfill the royal law according to the Scripture, "You shall love your neighbor as yourself," you are doing well" (James 2:8 ESV).

In Romans 12:9-13, Paul gives us the key to genuine Christian community which is love, and he points out 12 things we must do to express it. He states:

"Love must be sincere. Hate what is evil; cling to what is good. Be devoted to one another in brotherly love. Honor one another above yourselves. Never be lacking in zeal, but keep your spiritual fervor, serving the Lord. Be joyful in hope, patient in affliction, faithful in prayer. Share with God's people who are in need. Practice hospitality" (Romans 12:9-13 NIV).

- Love must be sincere. The word love here in the Greek is *agape*. It is an unconditional love, the love God has for us. This is the kind of love extended from one person to another through a committed relationship as with God/Christ. The Greek word for sincere is translated as *eilikrines*, meaning without hypocrisy or without play-acting. It's both honest and sincere.

- Hate what is evil. The Greek word for hate is *miseo*. It means to have a very strong intense feeling, to loathe, and look upon with horror.

- Cling to what is good. The word cling in Greek is *kollao*, which means to join or fasten together, to attach, to cement or glue together.

- Be devoted to one another in brotherly love. Brotherly love in Greek is *phileo* which means to be kind and affectionate towards another. This type of love is exemplified between siblings or close friends. We know that the American city of brotherly love is Philadelphia. The root of its name is *phileo*.

- Honor one another above yourselves. The Greek word for honor is *dokeo* which means to reverence, respect, or esteem. When we do this, we are showing true Christian love and care.

- Never be lacking in zeal. The Greek word for zeal is *zelos*, meaning enthusiastic devotion. We should not be lazy, slow-moving, sluggish, or lethargic in diligence.

- Keep your spiritual fervor, serving the Lord. The Greek word for fervor is *zeo*, meaning to be hot, to boil, or to set aflame. The believer's spirit is to be hot, boiling, and flaming for God/Jesus.

- Be joyful in hope. The Greek word for hope is *elpis*, meaning confident expectation. Our hope is God, and God is present, concerned, and caring.

- Be patient in affliction. The Greek word for patient is *hupomeno*, meaning abiding under, enduring, staying steadfastness, waiting for. God will do one of two things: either remove the trial or deliver you through the trial.

- Be faithful in prayer. The Greek word for faithful is *pistos*, this means to keep promises, give constant attention to, to be devoted and attentive.

- Share with God's people who are in need. The Greek word for sharing is *koinonia*, and it means joint participation, cooperation in a common interest or activity. Christians are to meet the needs of people unselfishly.

- Practice hospitality. The Greek word for hospitality is *philoxenos*. This means lover of strangers, showing care, and kindness. Hospitality means taking a genuine interest in others and making them feel welcomed and at ease.

Paul understands the command of Jesus from John 13:34 and Matthew 25:31-46. Here Paul shares with us that the Christian relationship is not for believers only, but is also extended to unbelievers as well. He starts with the key ingredient to our success is, "L.O.V.E." Paul stated,

"Love must be sincere" (v9). Sincere love goes further than politeness; it requires us to help others to become better people. It will also require personal involvement, and may require your time and money.

Jesus shows us over and over again the depth and quality of His relationship with us through His life, death, burial, and His resurrection. He said, "Greater love has no one than this, that a person will lay down his life for his friends" (John 15:13 NASB). The Apostle John stated, "By this we know what love is: Jesus laid down His life for us, and we ought to lay down our lives for our brothers" (1 John 3:16 BSB).

Genuine Christian community will never take place until we start to meet the needs of the people around us. We are instructed as Christians to give (ourselves, time, material items, and even money); because we know that God will pour out His love and blessing to everyone who exhibit love for others by gracious giving. Christians are to give as unto the Lord. One of our greatest reward is to participated in the ministry of Jesus Christ, and have the joy of seeing people blessed.

If we are to experience genuine Christian community we must look for people who need our love, and look for ways, along with the community of believers, to serve and show the love of Jesus to this world.

The Bible tells us, "Whoever speaks is to do so as one who is speaking actual words of God; whoever serves is to do so as one who is serving by the strength which God supplies; so that in all things God may be glorified through Jesus Christ, to whom belongs the glory and dominion forever and ever. Amen" (1 Peter 4:11 NASB).

PRAYER:

> Father God, help us to become one. Help us to be the Christian community You have called us to be, so that the world may see Your love and give You the glory. In Jesus' name – AMEN

Reflection Time:

1. Genuine Christian community will only happen when you meet the needs of the people around you. What step will you commit to take in order to create a better genuine Christian community?

   _____

   _____

   _____

   _____

   _____

   _____

   _____

   _____

   _____

2. What did Jesus say in John 13:34-35: _____

   _____

   _____

   _____

   _____

   _____

   _____

   _____

   _____

3. Genuine Christian community will never take place until we start meet the needs of the people around us. The Bible states: "_____

   _____

   _____

   _____

   _____ " (Luke 6:38 NIV).

4. The Bible tells us: "Whoever speaks is to do so as one who is speaking actual words of God; whoever serves is to do so as one who is serving by the strength which God supplies; so that in all things God may be glorified through Jesus Christ, to whom

belongs the glory and dominion forever and ever. Amen" (1 Peter 4:11 NASB).

What are the actions of genuine Christian community in this passage?

_____

_____

_____

_____

_____

_____

_____

_____

_____

_____

5. If we will experience genuine Christian community we must look for people who need our love, and look for ways that we, along with the community of believers, can serve and show the love of Jesus to this world.

    PRAY – and ask Jesus to give you one person you need to be a servant to.

    •   Name of person: _____

    •   Date started: _____

    •   Date completed: _____

6. Who will be the person that will hold you accountable in this area?

    _____

    _____

    _____

    _____

    _____

    _____

    _____

    _____

7. How can you apply what you've learned in this chapter to your personal life?

_____

_____

_____

_____

_____

_____

"The standard for a genuine Christian community is to "love." It's loving God and loving our neighbor as ourselves."

"Genuine Christian community will only happen when we begin to meet the needs of the people around us."

Chapter Seven

"The Christian Response to the World"

"Doing what Jesus would do"

"You have heard that it was said, 'An eye for an eye and a tooth for a tooth.' But I say to you, Do not resist the one who is evil. But if anyone slaps you on the right cheek, turn to him the other also. And if anyone would sue you and take your tunic, let him have your cloak as well. And if anyone forces you to go one mile, go with him two miles. Give to the one who begs from you, and do not refuse the one who would borrow from you. "You have heard that it was said, 'You shall love your neighbor and hate your enemy.' But I say to you, Love your enemies and pray for those who persecute you, so that you may be sons of your Father who is in heaven. For he makes his sun rise on the evil and on the good, and sends rain on the just and on the unjust" (Matthew 5:38-45 ESV).

This chapter will address one of the most important and sensitive areas in every Christian and non-Christian's life. This chapter deals primarily with the Christian response to the evil in the world we live in.

Almost everyone can think of a time when someone said something or did something to hurt us; whether intentional or unintentional, the hurt was real. Most of us can confirm that we've been lied on, talked about, misunderstood, mistreated. Some may be able to confirm accounts of physical, mental, and/or emotional abuse.

Interestingly, we can experience hurt from those who don't know us and also those who know us well. The truth is that some of these culprits are called friend, family, and/or church member. Shamefully, when I've experienced hurt; I haven't always responded well.

In the book of John, Jesus gives us fair warning about the evil in this world, the source, and the reason:

> "If the world hates you, keep in mind that it hated me first. If you belonged to the world, it would love you as its own. As it is, you do not belong to the world, but I have chosen you out of the world. That is why the world hates you. Remember the words I spoke to you: 'No servant is greater than his master." If they persecuted me, they will persecute you also. If they obeyed my teaching, they will obey yours also. They will treat you this way because of my name, for they do not know the One who sent me" (John 15:18-21 NIV).

The Apostle Paul warns Timothy and us in the book of Second Timothy, that everyone that pursues holiness will encounter opposition. Paul said:

> "Indeed, all who desire to live a godly life in Christ Jesus will be persecuted" (2 Timothy 3:12 BSB).

Before we read the next scripture, we must first understand the times and the mindset of the people in that time. In Old Testament times, to hate your enemies was practiced in practically every society. The Law of Moses said to love your neighbor; however, the Pharisees took this law and taught that the Jewish people should love those that were dear to them and hate all of Israel's enemies. So, the point Jesus was teaching the people in the Sermon on the Mount was foreign to the Israelites then hearing Jesus' message. In Jesus' sermon He taught how they (and we) should correctly respond to the evil acts of Satan and his followers.

> "You have heard that it was said, 'You shall love your neighbor and hate your enemy.' But I say to you, Love your enemies and pray for those who persecute you, so that you may be sons of your Father who is in heaven ..." (Matthew 5:43-45 ESV).

Jesus teaches to demonstrate God's love to everyone, even to our enemies. He raises the standard. Now this doesn't mean that we should allow people to abuse us! Even when they've been removed from our lives we can still love them with the love of Christ and pray that they will understand their error. Jesus told them and tells us that we're never more like God the Father than when we show love to others. Jesus teaches that we should both love our enemies and pray for them.

The Bible illustrates how Jesus taught not only in words regarding loving our enemies, but that He also demonstrated it. We see this very clearly at the crucifixion:

> "Now two others, who were criminals, were also being led away to be put to death with Him. And when they came to the place called The Skull, there they crucified Him and the criminals, one on the right and the other on the left. But Jesus was saying, "Father, forgive them; for they do not know what they are doing." And they cast lots, dividing His garments among themselves. And the people stood by, watching. And even the rulers were sneering at Him, saying, "He saved others; let Him save Himself if this is the Christ of God, His Chosen One." The soldiers also ridiculed Him, coming up to Him, offering Him sour wine, and saying, "If You are the King of the Jews, save Yourself" (Luke 23:32-37 NASB).

Let's look at how Jesus treated the people that crucified Him. First, Jesus, the Creator of all things allowed those He created to crucify Him unto an earthly death. He forgave them for doing it, and even prayed to the Father on their behalf while they were doing it. Jesus said that evil/mean people are blind with sin and they don't know what they're doing!

If we were to think of a time, situation, or person that hurt us, could we be like Jesus? He prayed for His enemies. Could you do that? The Bible tells us to "Be kind to one another, compassionate, forgiving each other, just as God in Christ also has forgiven you" (Ephesians 4:32 NASB).

> Note: We cannot control the actions of others; however, we can control our response. We must understand that all of us will be judged for our own actions and responses.

At the crucifixion, we clearly see Jesus doing just what He's taught us; how our response should be when someone hurts us deeply. He demonstrated true forgiveness and agape love.

We find Jesus teaching the disciples how to pray in Matthew chapter Six. We've come to know this prayer as "The Lord's Prayer." Now when we recite this prayer, it's always a healthy reflection to ask ourselves if we're doing what it's saying we should do.

> "And forgive us our debts, as we also have forgiven our debtors. And do not lead us into temptation, but deliver us from evil" (Matthew 6:12-13 NASB).

Think about it. When we say these words do we truly want Jesus to forgive us at the same level as we forgive others? The answer might be no. If our answer is no, then we want total forgiveness, forgiveness without a trace of wrong doing; but we're either unwilling to or incapable of extending this same kind of forgiveness to others. Jesus also says in this passage that forgiveness would lead us away from temptation and it would protect and deliver us from the devil and his evil.

The Apostle Paul shared with the Corinthian church how the devil uses unforgiveness against us. Paul says:

"If you forgive anyone, I also forgive him. And if I have forgiven anything, I have forgiven it in the presence of Christ for your sake, in order that Satan should not outwit us. For we are not unaware of his schemes" (2 Corinthians 2:10-11 BSB).

In Romans, the Apostle Paul teaches how churches are to properly respond to the evil in this world. He told them:

"Do not repay anyone evil for evil. Be careful to do what is right in the eyes of everyone. If it is possible, as far as it depends on you, live at peace with everyone. Do not take revenge, my friends, but leave room for God's wrath, for it is written: "It is mine to avenge; I will repay," says the Lord. On the contrary: "If your enemy is hungry, feed him; if he is thirsty, give him something to drink. In doing this, you will heap burning coals on his head." Do not be overcome by evil, but overcome evil with good" (Romans 12:17-21 NIV).

To respond this way is not an easy thing to do, because of our sinful nature. We all have a war going on inside of us; our flesh against our spirit and our human pride against godly humility. This is why we need a personal relationship with Jesus Christ and why we must surrender our lives and trust the Holy Spirit to give us the supernatural power we need to respond correctly to the evil in this world.

First, Paul teaches us that we are not to repay anyone evil for evil (v17) and we are not to seek revenge (v19).

- "'Do not seek revenge or bear a grudge against any of your people, but love your neighbor as yourself. I am the LORD" (Leviticus 19:18 BSB).

- The Apostle Peter teaches: "Do not repay evil with evil or insult with insult, but with blessing, because to this you were called so that you may inherit a blessing" (1 Peter 3:9 BSB).

Second, Paul teaches us that we are to live peaceably with all people, as far as it depends on us (v18).

- "When a man's ways please the LORD, He makes even his enemies to be at peace with him" (Proverbs 16:7 NKJV).

- "Let us therefore make every effort to do what leads to peace and to mutual edification" (Romans 14:19 NIV).

- ". . . Have salt in yourselves, and be at peace with one another" (Mark 9:50 ESV).

  Note: Paul said, "as far as it depends on us," this means the Christian should make the first move and the Christian should do everything within their power to make things right.

Third, Paul teaches that God will repay people for their evil against us; this is very important (v19).

- "That no one should take advantage of and defraud his brother in this matter, because the Lord is the avenger of all such, as we also forewarned you and testified" (1 Thessalonians 4:6 NKJV).

- "Do not say, "I will repay evil"; wait for the LORD, and he will deliver you" (Proverbs 20:22 ESV).

- "If your enemy is hungry, give him bread to eat, and if he is thirsty, give him water to drink, for you will heap burning coals on his head, and the LORD will reward you" (Proverbs 25:21-22 ESV).

And fourthly, Paul teaches us that we are to respond with kindness. We should respond by feeding others if they're hungry and giving them something to drink if they're thirsty; by doing this it's as if we're putting "burning coals on their heads." The burning coals are not coals of punishment, but rather conviction, because the goal here is repentance.

- "If your enemy is hungry, give him bread to eat, and if he is thirsty, give him water to drink" (Proverbs 25:21 ESV).

- "But I say to you who hear: Love your enemies, do good to those who hate you" (Luke 6:27 NKJV)

- "But I say unto you, Love your enemies, bless them that curse you, do good to them that hate you, and pray for them which despitefully use you, and persecute you" (Matthew 5:44 KJV).

Now, let's look at how Paul demonstrates the correct Christian response to the evil acts of this world.

> "Alexander the metalworker did me a great deal of harm. The Lord will repay him for what he has done. You too should be on your guard against him, because he strongly opposed our message. At my first defense, no one came to my support, but everyone deserted me. May it not be held against them. But the Lord stood at my side and gave me strength, so that through me the message might be fully proclaimed and all the Gentiles might hear it. And I was delivered from the lion's mouth. The Lord will rescue me from every evil attack and will bring me safely to his heavenly kingdom. To him be glory forever and ever. Amen" (2 Timothy 4:14-18 NIV).

Let's look at Paul's mindset. From the passage, we learn that Paul didn't try to get back at Alexander. What Paul did was warn the church about Alexander and left the situation in the hands of God to avenge him.

Paul may have even seen himself in Alexander the metalworker. He strongly opposed the message of the Gospel in his early years until God turned his life around. Maybe Paul remembered all the saints he had put in jail and the ones he had killed. The Bible lets us know that he was there when Stephen, the first martyr of the Gospel, was stoned to death. But what was more important was that Paul saw Stephen forgive and pray for the very people who stoned him to death.

Stephen prays for forgiveness for his killers.

> "Now hearing these things, they were cut to their hearts and began gnashing the teeth at him. But he being full of the Holy Spirit, having looked intently into heaven, saw the glory of God and Jesus standing at the right hand of God, and he said, "Behold, I see the heavens having been opened, and the Son of Man standing at the right hand of God." And having cried out with a loud voice, they held their ears and rushed upon him with one accord, and having cast him out of the city, began to stone him. And the witnesses laid aside their garments at the feet of a young man named Saul. And as they were stoning Stephen, he was calling out and saying, "Lord Jesus, receive my spirit." And having fallen on his knees, he cried in a loud voice, "Lord, do not place this sin to them." And having said this, he fell asleep." (Acts 7:54-60 BLB).

Stephen understood the teachings of Jesus and the Apostles. He understood that people would hate Christians and because he was a follower of Jesus, he knew his life might be in danger and he might even have to die. Stephen accepted this and understood that he must love, forgive, and pray for those who persecuted him.

Now let's look at the Christian or Christ-like response of the Apostles when they faced persecution.

In the book of Acts, we find a religious group called the Sadducees. This group were filled with jealousy because of the teachings of Jesus and the Apostles. The Bible tells us that the Apostles John and Peter were put in jail for healing a crippled man and for teaching the Gospel as Jesus instructed. We are told that God supernaturally released them and commanded them to go back to the temple courts and preach the Good News.

When the Sanhedrin found out that the Apostles were back teaching in the temple court, they made them come before them to be questioned by the High Priest. They said to Peter and John, "And they called them, and commanded them not to speak at all nor teach in the name of Jesus" (Acts 4:18 KJV). The Bible indicates that the Apostles stated, "We must obey God rather than men" (Acts 5:29 NASB). Their answer made the Sanhedrin want to put them to death. However, a Pharisee named Gamaliel stood up in the Sanhedrin gathering and addressed them saying, ". . . keep away from these men and let them alone; for if this plan or this work is of men, it will come to nothing; but if it is of God, you cannot overthrow it—lest you even be found to fight against God" (Acts 5:38-39 NKJV).

The Bible tells us that Gamaliel's speech persuaded them to spare the lives of the Apostles, so they had the Apostles beaten and before they let them go, they ordered them not to speak any longer in the name of Jesus before they let them go. The Bible states that the Apostles left the Sanhedrin, rejoicing because they had been counted worthy of suffering for the name of Jesus in the book of Acts chapter five, starting at verse seventeen through verse fourth-one.

Here we see the Christ-like response to injustice demonstrated by the Apostles. They were unjustly flogged, most likely receiving 39 lashes (the legal limit for lashing could not exceed 40 lashes in the Old Testament). The response to their unjust punishment was celebration that they were suffering for Christ. Though they were mistreated, they experienced supernatural joy. This is just one example of persecution towards Christians. During the time of Paul and even today, some are actually martyred for the faith.

We are also able to see from this example, Peter and John's persistent obedience to God. The scripture said that day after day, in the temple courts and from house to house, they never stopped teaching and proclaiming the good news that Jesus is the Christ (Acts 5:42 BLB).

Asking forgiveness for ourselves might be an easier task than forgiving others that have hurt us. We know that God loves us and He wants to set us free from any and all anger, bitterness, and pain. We can trust Him enough to surrender our hurts to Him.

So in your mind you may have asked the question; how do I get that supernatural power to forgive? God/Jesus knows that we can't do it in our own strength, so He has given every Christian the supernatural power to love, forgive, and live in peace through the person of the Holy Spirit.

> "These things I have spoken to you while being present with you. But the Helper, the Holy Spirit, whom the Father will send in My name, He will teach you all things, and bring to your remembrance all things that I said to you. Peace I leave with you, My peace I give to you; not as the world gives do I give to you. Let not your heart be troubled, neither let it be afraid" (John 14:25-27 NKJV).

Jesus wants all Christians to live in peace. In verse twenty-seven, He said that He would give us a supernatural peace that doesn't come from this world. He also said, "I have said these things to you, that in me you may have peace. In the world you will have tribulation. But take heart; I have overcome the world" (John 16:33 ESV).

Forgiveness, Forgive, Forgiving and Forgiven

Christian must understand that every person that have been on this earth is in need of forgiveness from God, because we have all committed sin. The Bible states, "Indeed, there is not a righteous person on earth who always does good and does not ever sin" (Ecclesiastes 7:20 NASB), also, "for all have sinned and fall short of the glory of God" (Romans 3:23 BLB). Because of our own actions, we all desperately need God's forgiveness. This is why we thank God for sending His Son Jesus Christ to die on the cross and for taking the penalty we deserved, which was death. Jesus was the atoning sacrifice for our sins, and because of his death and resurrection we can receive forgiveness by faith, through the grace and mercy of God. It's only through Jesus Christ that we can receive true forgiveness. The Bible says, "Therefore, my friend, I want you to know that through Jesus the forgiveness of sin is proclaimed to you" (Acts 13:38 NIV).

However, we must also understand that true reconciliation is impossible without genuine repentance. Unless we acknowledge our sins, we cannot enjoy true fellowship with the Father.

Forgiveness, Forgive, Forgiving, and Forgiven – What does forgiveness means?

- The word "forgive" means to wipe the slate clean, to pardon, to cancel a debt.

- The biblical meaning is "to not seek revenge!"

> "You have heard that it was said, 'An eye for an eye and a tooth for a tooth.' But I tell you not to resist an evil person. But whoever slaps you on your right cheek, turn the other to him also. If anyone wants to sue you and take away your tunic, let him have your cloak also. And whoever compels you to go one mile, go with him two" (Matthew 5:38-41 NKJV).

These verses talk about retribution or getting revenge. Jesus wants us to show the laws of grace and mercy by going the extra mile. Grace is God's unmerited favor given to someone or something that doesn't deserve it and mercy is God not punishing us as our sins deserve. This is what He wants us to extend to others in these situations.

Let's start with **the first phase of Forgiving which is Forgiveness:** Forgiveness is what we ask for when we are in the wrong and have offended someone. Asking for forgiveness is the beginning of our healing and it starts the process of bringing our relationships back into peace and humility.

We all must ask ourselves this question and answer it: has anyone ever hurt us more or worse than we ever hurt God? The answer is NO for all of us. Paul stated, "For all have sinned, and come short of the glory of God" (Romans 3:23 KJV).

Note: Jesus wants us to do all that is within our power to show the love of the Father.

"But I say to you that whoever is angry with his brother without a cause shall be in danger of the judgment. And whoever says to his brother, 'Raca (worthless)!' shall be in danger of the council. But whoever says, 'You fool!' shall be in danger of hell fire. Therefore, if you bring your gift to the altar, and there remember that your brother has something against you, leave your gift there before the altar, and go your way. First be reconciled to your brother, and then come and offer your gift (Matthew 5:22-24 NKJV).

When one of our relationships has gone wrong, the Christian should be the first to move to reconcile the broken relationship no matter who's at fault. The Bible tells us, "Make every effort to live in peace with all men and to be holy; without holiness no one will see the Lord" (Hebrews 12:14 NIV).

The second phase of Forgiving is Forgive: To forgive is a choice, a faith decision, not holding a sin against a person any longer. It is not based on standing, stature, value or worth, but on grace alone. Therefore, we should not confuse forgiveness with our emotions, because it's not a feeling.

- To forgive is more than just speaking the words, it must be sincere and from the heart. Our forgiveness must be patterned after the forgiveness God has given unto us and it must come with actions which indicate true forgiveness.

- We should always be willing to forgive our offenders, and even the repeat offenders. The apostle Peter asked Jesus a question: how many times shall I forgive our brother when they sin against us? Up to seven times? Jesus says to him, "I say to you not up to seven times, but up to seventy times seven" (Matthew 18:22 BLB)!

- We find that the principle of forgiveness is taught throughout the Bible. In Matthew 18:23-35, Jesus tells the Parable of the Unforgiving Servant:

"Therefore the kingdom of heaven may be compared to a king who wished to settle accounts with his servants. When he began to settle; one was brought to him who owed him ten thousand talents. And since he could not pay, his master ordered him to be sold, with his wife and children and all that he had, and payment to be made. So the servant fell on his knees, imploring him, 'Have patience with me, and I will pay you everything.' And out of pity for him, the master of that servant released him and forgave him the debt. But when that same servant went out, he found one of his fellow servants who owed him a hundred denarii, and seizing him, he began to choke him, saying, 'Pay what you owe.' So his fellow servant fell down and pleaded with him, 'Have patience with me, and I will pay you.' He refused and went and put him in prison until he should pay the debt. When his fellow servants saw what had taken place, they were greatly distressed, and they went and reported to their master all that had taken place. Then his master summoned him and said to him, 'You wicked servant! I forgave you all that debt because you pleaded with me. And should not you have had mercy on your fellow servant, as I had mercy on you?' And in anger his master delivered him to the jailers, until he should pay all his debt. So also my heavenly Father will do to every one of you, if you do not forgive your brother from your heart." (Matthew 18:23-35 ESV).

- Here Jesus' teaching was unmistakable to his disciples, He told them, "This is how My heavenly Father will treat each of you unless you forgive your brother from your heart" (Matthew 18:35 BSB).

The third phase of Forgiving is Forgiving: Forgiving is the process of aligning our will with our emotions. The key to successfully doing this is inviting the Lord Jesus into the process.

- The first thing we must do is PRAY! We must pray to the Lord Jesus to come with us on this with journey. We must also ask Him for the wisdom and for the courage it will take to be patient with others, and for the understanding we need as we work through the pain during the forgiveness process.

- The process of forgiving should begin with both parties understanding that a hurt exists and accept their responsibility for their own actions. The Bible tells us, "If your brother sins against you, go and confront him privately. If he listens to you, you have won your brother over" (Matthew 18:15 BSB).

- It's important for us to listen and try to understand what it's like for the other person, no matter how bad we feel.

- When we forgive someone the event or offense will still be a fact, but we no longer choose to hold it against them.

- The Bible tells us to bless those who persecute us (Romans 12:14 KJV), and love and pray for those who persecute us (Matthew 5:43-45 KJV). This means we are to intentionally pray for blessings on our offenders. By doing these things, it will allow the Holy Spirit to work in our hearts.

Note: This does not happen overnight; this process takes time. It may not always be possible for you to go to the other person. It may be wisdom to forgive the person without having to speak to them again if the encounter may be harmful to you. You're not responsible now or ever, for the response or actions of the other person. You're only responsible for you and your correct response.

The fourth phase of Forgiving is Forgiven: Forgiven is the conclusion. It's the end of the journey, the point, and place where our will and emotions come together. It is the place where we have true peace in our spirit.

- This process could also be called reconciliation; the completion of building a new, healthy relationship.

- When we forgive others, there is a freedom where we are no longer prisoner of our own anger and true restoration can occur in our hearts.

- This phase will be complete when we can rejoice with our offenders, and mean it from our hearts.

- As previously mentioned, this might not be possible depending on the offense, but the joy then is in knowing that your decision to forgive is pleasing to God and was the right thing to do.

- With Jesus, we can come to a point where forgiveness is a blessed way to live!

When Christians walk in love regarding the people that hurt them, it heaps conviction on them. They know that their reaction would not be the same if they were in our place. For them to see a Christian walk in love under adverse circumstances shows them we have something special they don't have . . . JESUS.

This means that we should live our lives as a sermon before the people of this world. This very well may be the only picture of God's love they have ever seen, and it will also allow us to minister in their lives with the goal of repentance and conversion.

Jesus and the Apostles have told us we would have conflict with others for various reasons and also for just simply being a Christian. We find throughout the scriptures that Jesus and the Apostles lived their lives just as the Christian's response should be when someone hurts us deeply; they demonstrated true forgiveness and Agape love. They also left us with some very comforting words:

> "Rejoice and be glad, for your reward is great in heaven, for so they persecuted the prophets who were before you" (Matthew 5:12 ESV).

> "Therefore, as God's chosen people, holy and dearly loved, clothe yourselves with compassion, kindness, humility, gentleness and patience. Bear with each other and forgive whatever grievances you may have against one another. Forgive as the Lord forgave you. And over all these virtues put on love, which binds them all together in perfect unity. Let the peace of Christ rule in your hearts, since as members of one body you were called to peace. And be thankful. Let the word of Christ dwell in you richly as you teach and admonish one another with all wisdom,

and as you sing psalms, hymns and spiritual songs with gratitude in your hearts to God. And whatever you do, whether in word or deed, do it all in the name of the Lord Jesus, giving thanks to God the Father through him" (Colossians 3:12-17 NIV).

Just remember, unforgiveness turns into resentment ... then into hate; and unforgiveness will also stops the flow of love, joy and peace.

PRAYER:

Father God, please cleanse my heart; help me to walk in love so it will be easy to forgive people. I thank you, Lord Jesus, for dying on the cross so my sins could and have been forgiven ... In Jesus' name – AMEN

Reflection Time:

1. Forgiveness, Forgive, Forgiving and Forgiven – What are the differences?

    a. Forgiveness is:

    _____

    _____

    _____

    _____

    _____

    b. Forgive is:

    _____

    _____

    _____

    _____

    _____

    c. Forgiving is:

    _____

    _____

    _____

    _____

    _____

    d. Forgiven is:

    _____

    _____

    _____

    _____

2. What person or people do I need to forgive?

    _____

    _____

    _____

    _____

    _____

    _____

3. What step(s) will I commit to take to create a better atmosphere with the people I have hurt and the people that have hurt me?

_____

_____

_____

_____

_____

_____

4. Who will be the person that will hold me accountable in this area?

_____

_____

_____

_____

_____

_____

5. How can I apply what I've learned in this chapter to my personal life?

_____

_____

_____

_____

_____

_____

"But they will treat you like this because of My name, since they do not know the One who sent Me" (John 15:21 BSB).

"Be kind to one another, compassionate, forgiving each other, just as God in Christ also has forgiven you" (Ephesians 4:32 NASB).

Chapter Eight

"The Christian View of SEX"

"Why is the right attitude about sex so important?"

"You have heard the commandment that says, 'You must not commit adultery.' But I say, anyone who even looks at a woman with lust has already committed adultery with her in his heart" (Matthew 5:27-28 NLT).

"It has been said, 'Anyone who divorces his wife must give her a certificate of divorce.' But I tell you that anyone who divorces his wife, except for sexual immorality, makes her the victim of adultery, and anyone who marries a divorced woman commits adultery" (Matthew 5:31-32 NIV).

Let me tell you up front this will be the longest chapter in this book, only because it is a very important and sensitive area in every Christian's and non-Christian's life.

"SEX" . . . it's not something we hear most Christians talking about. Some may say it is something that we should learn at home, and some may that think it's something we learn at school, and others may say that it is learned naturally. I would say to a certain extent it is true. Those areas could assist us in choosing a mate, which will be the second most important decision anyone will make in their whole life; second only to deciding if we will make Jesus the LORD of our life or not.

However, that is not what the world is telling us. The world says: sex, sex, sex and more sex; sex anytime, anywhere, and with anyone. The world uses sex for everything. To sell cars, to sell clothing, to sell sodas, to sell vacations, you name it they use it.

As I look around, I have found that teen pregnancy has become the norm, and in some cases I've found that teen pregnancy is down because of the growing level of homosexual activity in our society, both inside and outside of the church.

For most Christians, sex outside the marital union may be the area they have not surrendered over to God. It may very well be the number one biggest stumbling block for most Christians. On the other hand, there are some Christians that think that it's OK to have a sexual relationship outside the marriage union; however, that mindset is not based on the Word of God.

When we look at the Word of God we find that God has given all of mankind, the believer and the non-believer, the guidelines and instruction for all sexual relationships. He has given all of mankind the gift of sexual intimacy through the boundaries of a marital covenant ONLY!

Every true Christian in pursuit of holiness knows that our number one intimate relationship is with Jesus Christ and we understand that by surrendering everything to Him, our bodies are not our own. This is also why we are commanded to separate ourselves from the ways of the world.

As we look throughout the history of God's people we will find that God has always held His people to a higher standard than the people of the world. God's standard is, has been, and always will be holiness. The

Bible tells Christians that our bodies are the temple of the Holy Spirit, who is in every Christian, whom we have received from God (1 Corinthians 6:19 NKJV).

So, let's go back in history and look at the standard God has set for His people. In the book of Leviticus Chapter Eighteen we find God Himself instructing Moses on how to instruct the Israelites in all the areas of sexual relationships prohibited for all of mankind.

Prohibited Pagan Practices

"Then the LORD said to Moses, "Give the following instructions to the people of Israel. I am the LORD your God. So do not act like the people in Egypt, where you used to live, or like the people of Canaan, where I am taking you. You must not imitate their way of life. You must obey all my regulations and be careful to obey my decrees, for I am the LORD your God. If you obey my decrees and my regulations; you will find life through them. I am the LORD. "You must never have sexual relations with a close relative, for I am the LORD. "Do not violate your father by having sexual relations with your mother. She is your mother; you must not have sexual relations with her. "Do not have sexual relations with any of your father's wives, for this would violate your father. "Do not have sexual relations with your sister or half-sister, whether she is your father's daughter or your mother's daughter, whether she was born into your household or someone else's. "Do not have sexual relations with your granddaughter, whether she is your son's daughter or your daughter's daughter, for this would violate yourself. "Do not have sexual relations with your stepsister, the daughter of any of your father's wives, for she is your sister. "Do not have sexual relations with your father's sister, for she is your father's close relative. "Do not have sexual relations with your mother's sister, for she is your mother's close relative. "Do not violate your uncle, your father's brother, by having sexual relations with his wife, for she is your aunt. "Do not have sexual relations with your daughter-in-law; she is your son's wife, so you must not have sexual relations with her. "Do not have sexual relations with your brother's wife, for this would violate your brother. "Do not have sexual relations with both a woman and her daughter. And do not take her granddaughter, whether her son's daughter or her daughter's daughter, and have sexual relations with her. They are close relatives, and this would be a wicked act. "While your wife is living, do not marry her sister and have sexual relations with her, for they would be rivals. "Do not have sexual relations with a woman during her period of menstrual impurity. "Do not defile yourself by having sexual intercourse with your neighbor's wife. "Do not permit any of your children to be offered as a sacrifice to Molech, for you must not bring shame on the name of your God. I am the LORD. "Do not practice homosexuality, having sex with another man as with a woman. It is a detestable sin. "A man must not defile himself by having sex with an animal. And a woman must not offer herself to a male animal to have intercourse with it. This is a perverse act. "Do not defile yourselves in any of these ways, for the people I am driving out before you have defiled themselves in all these ways. Because the entire land has become defiled; I am punishing the people who live there. I will cause the land to vomit them out. You must obey all my decrees and regulations. You must not commit any of these detestable sins. This applies both to native-born Israelites and to the foreigners living among you. "All these detestable activities are practiced by the people of the land where I am taking you, and this is how the land has become defiled. So do not defile the land and give it a reason to vomit you out, as it will vomit out the people who live there now. Whoever commits any of these detestable sins will be cut off from the community of Israel. So obey my instructions, and do not defile yourselves by committing any of these detestable practices that were committed by the people who lived in the land before you. I am the LORD your God" (Leviticus 18:1-30 NLT).

Let's look at these areas of sexual relationships that God has prohibited for ALL of mankind and the areas which the Bible says are detestable sins before God the Father:

- Verse 6 – He prohibited sexual relations with a close relative: (mother v7; sister v6; your children, v9; grandchildren v10; aunt, v12; daughter-in-law, v15; sister-in-law, v16).

- Verse 17 – He prohibited sexual relations with both a mother and her daughter.

- Verse 19 – He prohibited sexual relations with any woman on her monthly period.

- Verse 20 – He prohibited sexual relations with a neighbor's spouse.

- Verse 21 – He prohibited giving children as human sacrifices for sex gods.

- Verse 22 – He prohibited all homosexual relationships.

- Verse 23 – He prohibited bestiality (a sexual relationship with an animal).

These sexual relationships were common in most pagan cultures and religions. In today's society, some of these practices are being taken lightly and some groups are even trying to make them acceptable. But for the Christian, God has given us His guidelines for healthy sexual relationships and He has also given us the list of sexual relationships that are worldly and detestable before Him. He tells us that if anyone practices these detestable lifestyles, we should cut off all contact with these people, and have no relationships with them (Leviticus 18:29-30 NLT).

Let's look at what Jesus has to say about sex. We find that when Jesus was teaching at the Sermon on the Mount, He preached on the areas of lusting, marital unfaithfulness and adultery.

First lusting:

> "You have heard the commandment that says, 'You must not commit adultery.' But I say, anyone who even looks at a woman with lust has already committed adultery with her in his heart" (Matthew 5:27-28 NLT).

Here we find Jesus' teaching on the law against adultery which is the seventh Commandment (Exodus 20:14 and Deuteronomy 5:18 KJV). He taught them that the act of lusting was as bad as the act itself. The Apostle James put it this way; "But each one is tempted when he is drawn away by his own desires and enticed. Then, when desire has conceived, it gives birth to sin; and sin, when it is full-grown, brings forth death" (James 1:14-15 NKJV).

Second marital unfaithfulness:

> "It has been said, 'Anyone who divorces his wife must give her a certificate of divorce.' But I tell you that anyone who divorces his wife, except for marital unfaithfulness, causes her to become an adulterous, and anyone who marries the divorced woman commits adultery" (Matthew 5:31-32 NIV).

The Bible tells us that God hates divorce (Malachi 2:16 NKJV), however, we find that the people of that time had a wrong understanding of the Law of Moses. Moses provided the certificate of divorce as an acknowledgment to protect the women from falling under the penalty of adultery, which was punished by stoning to death.

Here Jesus teaches that spouses should not break up any marriage because it would cause the other spouse to become adulterous because of their actions.

Here we also find that Jesus teaches that we should not misuse our gift of sexual intimacy outside the boundaries of our marriage covenant by committing adultery. We should not have the lustful spirit of adultery, and we should cause no one else to commit adultery by our actions. However, the most important thing Jesus pointed out to us was that it is a heart issue.

As we look at the Apostle Paul, we will find that he had a lot to say about the importance of holiness in an unhealthy, unbiblical sexual world.

With the sexual conduct of the people in Paul's day we found there were distorted views about women, sex, and marriage. We found the words of Paul concerning sex and marriage were desperately needed in his day and time and it is also needed today. So, let's see what the Word of God has to say to us through the Apostle Paul.

The Corinthians' sexual behavior very well may have been the world's worst at that day and time. Paul tells the members of this church:

> "Do you not know that the wicked will not inherit the kingdom of God? Do not be deceived: Neither the sexually immoral, nor idolaters, nor adulterers, nor men who submit to or perform homosexual acts, nor thieves, nor the greedy, nor drunkards, nor verbal abusers, nor swindlers, will inherit the kingdom of God. And that is what some of you were. But you were washed, you were sanctified, you were justified, in the name of the Lord Jesus Christ and by the Spirit of our God (1 Corinthians 6:9-11 BSB).

Paul expressed to them that the way they were living was not in line with kingdom living and that their behavior would keep them out of heaven (v9 and 10). Paul also warned them about the traps of the world by saying, "Do not be deceived."

Next Paul called the sins by name, and we find these four sexual offenders:

- The sexually immoral
- The adulterers
- The prostitutes
- The homosexual offenders

But thanks be to our Lord and Savior Jesus Christ, that if ANY sexual offender would repent from their sinful lifestyle and seek the Lord Jesus with their whole heart, He will wash, sanctify, and justify you by His name and by the Spirit of our God.

As we read Paul's letter to the church in Rome, we find that the Roman sexual ethic was no better than the church in Corinth. Paul told the Roman church that their theology and actions were not in line with the truth of God's Word about God's guidelines in sexual behavior. Paul reminded them that God has made His plan clear to them, and they would be without excuse when God's wrath is poured out on them because they had exchanged the truth of God for a lie.

"The wrath of God is being revealed from heaven against all the godlessness and wickedness of people, who suppress the truth by their wickedness, since what may be known about God is plain to them, because God has made it plain to them. For since the creation of the world God's invisible qualities—his eternal power and divine nature—have been clearly seen, being understood from what has been made, so that people are without excuse. For although they knew God, they neither glorified him as God nor gave thanks to him, but their thinking became futile and their foolish hearts were darkened. Although they claimed to be wise, they became fools and exchanged the glory of the immortal God for images made to look like a mortal human being and birds and animals and reptiles. Therefore, God gave them over in the sinful desires of their hearts to sexual impurity for the degrading of their bodies with one another. They exchanged the truth about God for a lie, and worshiped and served created things rather than the Creator—who is forever praised. Amen. Because of this, God gave them over to shameful lusts. Even their women exchanged natural sexual relations for unnatural ones. In the same way the men also abandoned natural relations with women and were inflamed with lust for one another. Men committed shameful acts with other men, and received in themselves the due penalty for their error. Furthermore, just as they did not think it worthwhile to retain the knowledge of God, so God gave them over to a depraved mind, so that they do what ought not to be done. They have become filled with every kind of wickedness, evil, greed and depravity. They are full of envy, murder, strife, deceit and malice. They are gossips, slanderers, God-haters, insolent, arrogant and boastful; they invent ways of doing evil; they disobey their parents; they have no understanding, no fidelity, no love, no mercy. Although they know God's righteous decree that those who do such things deserve death, they not only continue to do these very things but also approve of those who practice them" (Romans 1:18-32 NIV).

As we look at the wrath (judgment) of God on these sexually immoral Romans, we see that God's punishment began for those individuals here on earth. In verse 18 Paul said, "The wrath of God is being revealed;" meaning it is a present manifestation of God's wrath on all of creation, because of the rejection of God's standards and the establishing their own.

Because of their sexually immoral relationships the Bible states that God gave them over three times (v24, 26, and 28) telling us how God's wrath works. He will allow an individual to damn themselves by continuing on their self-destructive path or He removes His hand of protection from them.

- "Therefore God gave them over in the sinful desires of their hearts to sexual impurity for the degrading of their bodies with one another" (Romans 1:24 NIV).

- "Because of this, God gave them over to shameful lusts. Even their women exchanged natural relations for unnatural ones" (Romans 1:26 NIV).

- "Furthermore, since they did not think it worthwhile to retain the knowledge of God, he gave them over to a depraved mind; to do what ought not to be done" (Romans 1:28 NIV).

Jude also writes and tells us about what history demonstrates and the judgment of God on sexually immoral people. Jude points to Sodom and Gomorrah and says: "And don't forget Sodom and Gomorrah and their neighboring towns, which were filled with immorality and every kind of sexual perversion. Those cities were destroyed by fire and serve as a warning of the eternal fire of God's judgment" (Jude 1:7 NLT).

We have found there are basically four main areas of sexual relationships clearly forbidden throughout the Bible and these four forbidden areas are adultery, fornication, sexual immorality, and homosexuality. We have also found there is a fifth area known as masturbation.

Adultery:

The word adulterer, adulterers, adulteress, adulteresses, adulteries, adulterous, and adultery or topic of adultery is mention about sixty-six times throughout the Bible.[13] It is when one or both persons step outside of their marriage covenant and have a sexual relationship with someone other than their spouse. The Bible states:

- "'If a man commits adultery with his neighbor's wife, both the man and the woman who have committed adultery must be put to death" (Leviticus 20:10 NLT).

- "He who commits adultery lacks judgment; whoever does so destroys himself" (Proverbs 6:32 BSB).

- "For the One having said, "You shall not commit adultery," also said, "You shall not murder." But if you do not commit adultery, but do commit murder, you have become a transgressor of the Law" (James 2:11 BLB).

Fornication:

The topic or word fornication, fornications, fornicator, or fornicators is talked about forty-four times throughout the Bible.[14] Fornication is the act of having sex without a marriage covenant; it is the act of having sex when both persons are single. The Bible states:

- "Therefore put to death your members which are on the earth: fornication, uncleanness, passion, evil desire, and covetousness, which is idolatry" (Colossians 3:5 NKJV).

- "But fornication and all uncleanness or covetousness, let it not even be named among you, as is fitting for saints" (Ephesians 5:3 NKJV).

- "Now the works of the flesh are evident, which are: adultery, fornication, uncleanness, lewdness," (Galatians 5:19 NKJV).

Note: Paul commands us to flee (run from) fornication (1 Corinthians 6:18 KJV), because he called it idolatry, which is a self-worship.

Sexual Immorality:

The word "sexual immorality" is a New International Version Bible word, which shows up 20 times. In the King James Version is shows up as "fornication," which shows up 32 times. In the New King James Version it is called it "lewdness," which shows up 16 times. The New America Standard uses the word "immorality," which shows up 22 times. And the New Living Translation Version uses the word "sexual immorality," which shows up 14 times. So, we find this topic of sexual immorality is talked about over 20 times throughout the various versions of the Bible. [15]

Sexual immorality is an act of arousing or stimulating a sexual emotion and desire in yourself or someone else. This act is better known as foreplay; it's doing everything up to the act of sex, such as oral sex, masturbation, erotic stimulation with other body parts such as hands, fingers, feet, toys, etc. Paul told the Corinthian church that if they cannot control themselves, they should get married, for it is better for them to marry than to burn with passion or sexual desires (1 Corinthians 7:9 NKJV).

Sexual immorality starts off as simply embracing a person (erotic hugging, passionate kissing). The second level of sexual immorality moves to caressing and the rubbing of body parts, with the clothes on. And then the third level of sexual immorality is stimulation and the removal of clothing, stopping short of the act of sex. The Bible states:

- "It is God's will that you should be sanctified: that you should avoid sexual immorality" (1 Thessalonians 4:3 NIV).

- "Do you not know that the unrighteous will not inherit the kingdom of God? Do not be deceived. Neither fornicators, nor idolaters, nor adulterers, nor homosexuals, nor sodomites" (1 Corinthians 6:9 NKJV).

- "Now the works of the flesh are evident, which are sexual immorality, impurity, sensuality, idolatry, sorcery, enmities, strife, jealousy, outbursts of anger, contentions, dissensions, factions, envyings, drunkennesses, carousing, and things like these, as to which I forewarn you, even as I warned before, that those doing such things will not inherit God's kingdom" (Galatians 5:19-21 BLB).

- "Do you not know that your bodies are members of Christ? Shall I then take the members of Christ and make them members of a prostitute? Never! Or do you not know that he who is joined to a prostitute becomes one body with her? For, as it is written, "The two will become one flesh" (1 Corinthians 6:15-16 ESV)? For it is said, "The two will become one flesh" (Mark 10:8 NKJV).

- Paul commands us to flee from sexual immorality. He says it's because all our other sins we commit are outside our bodies, but a sexual sin is against our own body (1 Corinthians 6:18 KJV).

Note: Paul stated to the Corinthian church about their sexual immorality; "It is good for a man not to touch a woman (have sexual relations)" (1 Corinthians 7:1 NKJV).

Masturbation:

The question is, is masturbation a sin? "YES!" Masturbation is a self-gratifying act that only pleases the individual and it does not glorify God. It is an act of a person having sex with oneself. It generally occurs when a person is having sexual thoughts about someone about whom they should not be having sexual thoughts, which is "lust of the flesh." We have Onan in the book of Genesis as an example of someone misusing his semen by putting it on the ground.

- "But Onan knew that the offspring would not be his. So, whenever he went in to his brother's wife he would waste the semen on the ground, so as not to give offspring to his brother. And what he did was wicked in the sight of the LORD, and he put him to death also" (Genesis 38:9-10 ESV).

- In Matthew chapter five Jesus stated: "You have heard that it was said, 'Do not commit adultery.' But I tell you that anyone who looks at a woman to lust after her has already committed adultery with her in his heart. If your right eye causes you to sin, gouge it out and throw it away. It is better for you to lose one part of your body than for your whole body to be thrown into hell. And if your right hand causes you to sin, cut it off and throw it away. It is better for you to lose one part of your body than for your whole body to depart into hell" (Matthew 5:27-30 BSB). Here in verses 29 and 30, Jesus very well may be talking about the act of looking at pornography and the act of masturbation. If so, He is stating that one should take extreme measures to avoid these types of sin.

Note: Onan's only desire was to please himself; he had no desire in fulfilling God's plan for sex. Therefore, masturbation is a self-gratifying act that only pleases oneself.

Homosexuality:

The words homosexual and homosexuality did not appear in the Bible until 1973. The first time it appeared in an American Bible was the New International Version (NIV), and it is only found in the Bible a few times under this name.

Paul uses the Greek word arsenkoitai in 1 Corinthians 6:9-10 in the NIV, which shows up as homosexual in the New International Version of the Bible, however in the New King James Version it has been translated as abusers of themselves with mankind.

We all know that homosexuality is the act of the same gender having sex (male to male or female to female relationships). The Bible states:

- "Do not practice homosexuality, having sex with another man as with a woman. It is a detestable sin" (Leviticus 18:22 NLT).

- "If a man practices homosexuality, having sex with another man as with a woman, both men have committed a detestable act. They must both be put to death, for they are guilty of a capital offense" (Leviticus 20:13 NLT).

- "For the sexually immoral, for those practicing homosexuality, for slave traders and liars and perjurers—and for whatever else is contrary to the sound doctrine" (1 Timothy 1:10 NIV).

- "Don't you realize that those who do wrong will not inherit the Kingdom of God? Don't fool yourselves. Those who indulge in sexual sin, or who worship idols, or commit adultery, or are male prostitutes, or practice homosexuality" (1 Corinthians 6:9 NLT).

For the past few pages in this chapter we have looked at all the prohibited sexual relationships which God has outlined throughout His Word. So, we must now answer the question: what is God's view and plan for our lives concerning sexual relationships?

God's plan for sex is clearly defined in His Word (Bible). In the first book of the Bible, Genesis, the first chapter, God created man in His own image; in the image of God He created him; male and female. One of the first things we notice is that even our sexuality relates us to the image of God, "male and female he created them" (Genesis 1:27 KJV).

The second thing we notice is that the act of sex is in a covenant relationship. The Bible states:

• "For this reason a man will leave his father and mother and be united to his wife, and they will become one flesh. And the man and his wife were both naked, and they were not ashamed" (Genesis 2:24-25 BSB).

One flesh refers to the uniting of two monogamous people through sex. This verse makes it clear that the Lord God wants us to wait and have sex in a covenant relationship. Sex is a gift of God that is confined to the institutes of a marriage union. The Bible states:

• "Marriage should be honored by all, and the marriage bed kept pure, for God will judge the adulterer and all the sexually immoral" (Hebrews 13:4 NIV).

• "It is God's will that you should be sanctified: that you should avoid sexual immorality; that each of you should learn to control his own body in a way that is holy and honorable, not in passionate lust like the heathen, who do not know God" (1 Thessalonians 4:3-5 NIV).

• "Drink water from your own cistern, And running water from your own well. Should your fountains be dispersed abroad, Streams of water in the streets? Let them be only your own, And not for strangers with you. Let your fountain be blessed, And rejoice with the wife of your youth. As a loving deer and a graceful doe, Let her breasts satisfy you at all times; And always be enraptured with her love. For why should you, my son, be enraptured by an immoral woman, And be embraced in the arms of a seductress" (Proverbs 5:15-20 NKJV)?

So why is the subject of sex so important? It's important because it's: Physical, Spiritual, Emotional, and Psychological. Sex is powerful and it affects us in more ways than some may think.

Physical:

- One reason sex is physical is because it's for procreation. The Bible tells us that God blessed the man and the woman and commanded them to "Be fruitful and multiply" (Genesis 1:28 KJV).

- We find that one of the biggest differences between men and women is that men experience sex as a legitimate physical need. Just as our body tells us when we're thirsty or hungry, the male's body tells him when he needs a sexual release. Men's sexual desire is impacted by what's around him but is determined by biological factors, specifically the presence of testosterone in his body.

- Women don't experience their physical drive for sex in the same way men; there is no buildup that demands release. However, hormone fluctuations drive women's sexuality. Female sexual hormones are highly different in two ways: the female reproductive cycle and a part of the brain called the hypothalamus.

- However, far too often we hook up with someone only because we're physically attracted to them.

Spiritual:

- One reason sex is spiritual is because the Bible tells us that we become one spiritually with the person with whom we have a sexual relationship, which creates a Soul Tie, The two will become one flesh in Genesis 2:24; Matthew 19:5; Mark 10:8; Ephesians 5:31; and 1 Corinthians 6:16 (KJV). Paul said this even happens with a prostitute: "Do you not know that he who unites himself with a prostitute is one with her in body? For it is said, "The two will become one flesh." Basically, every time you have sexual intercourse with someone you become one flesh with that person and with everyone that person has had sex with.

- On a positive note, sex is spiritual because it fulfills scripture. The Word of God states, "But because of the temptation to sexual immorality, each man should have his own wife and each woman her own husband. The husband should give to his wife her conjugal rights, and likewise the wife to her husband. For the wife does not have authority over her own body, but the husband does. Likewise the husband does not have authority over his own body, but the wife does. Do not deprive one another, except perhaps by agreement for a limited time, that you may devote yourselves to prayer; but then come together again, so that Satan may not tempt you because of your lack of self-control" (1 Corinthians 7:2-5 ESV).

Note: Paul said, let each man have his own wife, and let each woman have her own husband (v 2). Let the husband fulfill his duty to his wife, and likewise also the wife to her husband (v 3). Neither the husband nor the wife has authority over their own bodies (v 4).

- Another biblical reason is because of our personal spirit connection. The Bible states, "Has not the LORD made them one, having a portion of the Spirit? And why one? Because He seeks godly offspring. So, guard yourselves in your spirit and do not break faith with the wife of your youth" (Malachi 2:15 BSB).

Emotional:

- One reason sex is emotional is because it can affect various physical feelings such as moods, temperament, disposition, personality, and motivation which can even affect hormones. Just look at King David, he stated, "O Lord, do not rebuke me in Your wrath, Nor chasten me in Your hot displeasure! For Your arrows pierce me deeply, And Your hand presses me down. There is no soundness in my flesh Because of Your anger, Nor any health in my bones Because of my sin. For my iniquities have gone over my head; Like a heavy burden they are too heavy for me. My wounds are foul and festering Because of my foolishness. I am troubled, I am bowed down greatly; I go mourning all the day long. For my loins are full of inflammation, And there is no soundness in my flesh. I am feeble and severely broken; I groan because of the turmoil of my heart" (Psalm 38:1-8 NKJV).

- When it's comes to having sex outside the marriage covenant we may not get a sexually transmitted disease or get pregnant, but no one is immune from getting hurt. See, most people who have sex outside the marriage covenant often experience emotional difficulties such as: the regret of losing their virginity; anger towards their partner; the discomfort of felling used; and/or the feeling of guilt of letting down their parents or breaking their commitment to God. If you talk to a group of sexually active female teens, some would admit that they felt bad about themselves for giving in to the sexual temptation and that having sex leaves emotional scars.

Psychological:

- One reason sex is psychological is because it can also cause an individual to have an unstable physical reaction or an unstable attitude in sex. This may very well be the attitude of the rapists and stalkers. In the Bible, we have the story of Amnon and Tamar, two of King David kids. It states, "Amnon became so obsessed with his sister Tamar that he made himself ill. She was a virgin, and it seemed impossible for him to do anything to her," meaning that his lust for her moved him to the point of sickness (2 Samuel 13:2 NIV). This chapter also tells us Amnon raped his sister Tamar, and after it was all over, he hated her with an intense hatred; that he hated her more than he had loved her in the beginning.

Note: This tells us that sex outside of God's guidelines can lead to destruction and disaster of lives and relationships.

Sex outside of marriage starts a chain reaction: first comes the sexual intercourse, then the guilt, the self-deception, then the desertion. Spiritually what happens to us is that we're separated from God, we move away from the Church, and we move away from true righteousness.

These are some reasons why Paul told us to "present your bodies as a living sacrifice, holy and acceptable to God, which is your spiritual worship" (Romans 12:1 ESV). Paul tells us, "Do not conform any longer to the pattern of this world, but be transformed by the renewing of your mind" (Romans 12:2 NIV). It is important for all of us to renew our minds, because the un-renewed mind is infected with STD's. STD's are "Stinking Thinking Disorder." A "stinking thinking disorder" is what the Bible call a depraved mind (Romans 1:28 BLB).

Let's look at the facts and statistics of Stinking Thinking Disorder (STD):

The statistics of cohabitation:[16]

- More than eight out of ten couples who live together will break-up either before the wedding or end in divorce.
- About 45% of people that cohabitate (live together) do not get married, and the couples who get married after living together are 50% more likely to end in divorce.
- Only 12% of couples who have begun their relationship with cohabitation end up with a marriage lasting 10 or more years.
- Couples living together are 62 times more likely to suffer abuse from their partner.

The statistics of couples that wait to have sex:[17]

Brigham Young University recently conducted a large study of 2,035 married individuals, aiming to determine which factors contribute to a "happy" marriage. According to the study findings, the couples that waited until marriage to have sex have these benefits:

- 22% higher relationship stability
- 20% higher relationship satisfaction
- 15% better sex ("higher sexual quality of the relationship")
- 12% better communication.

Note: "Good things come to couples who wait"

The statistics of teenagers that said, "YES," they are having sex:[18]

- 24% of 14-year-olds said YES.

- 42% of 15-year-olds said YES.

- 42% of 16-year-olds said YES.

- 60% of 17-year-olds said YES.

- And 56% of teenagers said that they had sex in their parents' home the first time . . . while the parents were home.

The statistics of Americans that get a STD:[19]

- Nineteen million new sexually transmitted infections (STIs) occur each year, almost half among young people ages 15 to 24.

- 10,000 teens are infected by STIs per day, one every eight seconds!

- One out of every four sexually active teens has an STI, and one in two sexually active youth will contract an STI by age 25.

- In 2006, adolescents and young adults 13-29 years old accounted for the greatest percentage of new HIV infections (34%) than any other age group.

- African-American young adults are disproportionately affected by HIV infection, accounting for 60% of HIV/AIDS diagnoses in 13 to 24-year old's in 2006.

- Teens are also more likely to develop precancerous growths because of HPV infection, and these growths are more likely to develop into invasive cancer.

- Although youth are at higher risk for acquiring STIs, only 1/3 of sexually active teens age 15 to 17, and 1/2 of sexually active young adult's ages 18 to 24 said that they have been tested for STIs.

- Less than half of adults ages 18 to 44 have ever been tested for an STD/STI other than HIV/AIDS.

Note: More than $8 billion is spent each year to diagnose and treat STDs/STIs and their complications. This figure does not include HIV.

The statistics of Unplanned Pregnancy:[20]

- According to U.S. Health and Human Services, 1 in 3 girls will get pregnant before she turns twenty. Almost 1 million teens get pregnant every year. Most pregnancies are unplanned and cause turmoil for the teen mother, the baby's father, and their families.

- About 80% of women and teens that don't use contraception or birth control will get pregnant within a year. This high statistic leads so many mothers to getting pregnant unexpectedly. Unfortunately, about 25% pregnancies will cause adoption and about 27% of all teenage pregnancies result in abortion.

The Positive Statistics about Sex:

Ten Great Health Benefits of having Sex:[21]

- Having sex could lower your stress and your blood pressure. That finding comes from a Scottish study of 24 women and 22 men who kept records of their sexual activity. The researchers put them in stressful situations, such as speaking in public and doing math out loud, and checked their blood pressure.

- Having sex boosts immunity: Studies show that having sex once or twice a week has been linked with higher levels of an antibody called immunoglobulin A or IgA, which can protect you from getting colds and other infections.

- Sex burns calories: Thirty minutes of sex burns 85 calories or more. It may not sound like much, but it adds up: 42 half-hour sessions will burn 3,570 calories, more than enough to lose a pound.

- Sex improves heart health: Having sex may be good for your heart. A 20-year-long British study shows that men who had sex twice or more a week were half as likely to have a fatal heart attack than men who had sex less than once a month. And although some older folks may worry that the sex could cause a stroke, that study found no link between how often men had sex and how likely they were to have a stroke.

- Having sex gives better self-esteem: don't have lots of sex to feel good about yourself. Your self-esteem is all about you -- not someone else. But if you're already feeling good about yourself, a great sex life may help you feel even better.

- Deeper intimacy: Having sex and orgasms boosts levels of the hormone oxytocin, the love hormone, which helps people bond and build trust. Higher oxytocin levels have also been linked with a feeling of generosity.

- Sex may reduce body pain: It boosts your body's painkillers, called endorphins. So if your headache, arthritis pain, or PMS symptoms seem to improve after sex that may be why.

- Having sex may make prostate cancer less likely: a study published in the Journal of the American Medical Association, found that men with 21 or more ejaculations a month were less likely to get prostate cancer than those who had four to seven ejaculations per month.

- Having sex can strengthen pelvic floor muscles: For women, doing pelvic floor muscle exercises called Kegels may mean they may enjoy more pleasure -- and, as a perk, less chance of incontinence later in life.

- Having sex helps us get better sleep: The oxytocin released during orgasm also promotes sleep, research shows. Getting enough sleep has also been linked with a host of other health perks, such as a healthy weight and better blood pressure.

The Life Expectancy of having Sex:[22]

- Sex not only helps by keeping close human contact in your life, it may even add 3-8 years to your life. While not a great deal of research has been done among older adults, it seems that people with frequent orgasms do live longer. This makes sense -- an orgasm releases chemical in your body that cause relaxation and pleasure. These chemicals, if released often enough, may counteract the negative effects of stress.

In the Bible, we found that sex is a biblical part of God's good creation. Its function is for ministering to one's mate through a marriage covenant of physical affection for procreation. It will also create a union of oneness of body, mind, and spirit between a husband and his wife.

We also found that sexuality and spirituality are closely related. Paul calls for each of us who know God through Jesus Christ to elevate our sexuality standard to the one set by God. When we make sexuality an expression of our spirituality to the glory of God, it's ultimately for our good.

As we pursue holiness, we must remember the words of Paul: "Or do you not know that your body is a temple of the Holy Spirit in you, whom you have from God? And you are not your own" (1 Corinthians 6:19 BLB), and he also told us, ". . . Every sin, whatever if a man might do, is outside the body, but the one sinning sexually sins against the own body" (1 Corinthians 6:18 BLB).

Therefore, the Christian that is pursuing holiness must also pursue sexual purity as well! Paul states, "It is God's will that you should be sanctified: that you should avoid sexual immorality, that each of you should learn to control your own body in a way that is holy and honorable" (1 Thessalonians 4:3-4 NIV).

PRAYER:

Father God, please help up through the power of the Holy Spirit to live our lives in line with the commands you have put in place when it comes to sex. Please help every person that is struggling in this area. In Jesus' name – AMEN

Reflection Time:

1. Why is having the right attitude about sex so important?

    _____

    _____

    _____

    _____

    _____

    _____

    _____

    _____

2. The four sexual offenders are:
    a. _____.
    b. _____.
    c. _____.
    d. _____.

3. The question is, is masturbation a sin? And Why?

    _____

    _____

    _____

    _____

    _____

    _____

    _____

    _____

4. What step will you commit to take to keep yourself holy in this area?

    _____

    _____

    _____

    _____

    _____

    _____

5. Sex outside of marriage starts a chain reaction:
   a. _____.
   b. _____.
   c. _____.

6. What happens spiritually? _____
   And _____.

7. It is important for all of us to renew our minds, because the un-renewed mind is infected with STD's. What is a STD? _____.

8. Is masturbation or pornography a sin? Explain your answer.

   _____
   _____
   _____
   _____
   _____
   _____
   _____
   _____

9. Give one reasons sex is psychological?

   _____
   _____
   _____
   _____
   _____
   _____
   _____

10. Give one reasons sex is spiritual?

   _____
   _____
   _____
   _____
   _____

_____

_____

11. How can you apply what you've learned in this chapter to your personal life?

_____

_____

_____

_____

_____

_____

_____

_____

12. Who will be the person that will hold you accountable in this area?

_____

_____

_____

_____

_____

_____

_____

_____

_____

 When it comes to SEX – are you following God's guide lines or Satan's?

Sex is Physical, it's Spiritual, it's Emotional, and it's Psychological!

Chapter Nine

"Worship and Praise"

"In the same way, let your light shine before others, so that they may see your good works and give glory to your Father who is in heaven" (Matthew 5:16 ESV).

Back in chapter two we talked about the purpose of God creating man. We said that the first was to fellowship with Him, the second purpose was to serve and worship Him, and the third was to live eternally with Him. As we move throughout the rest of this chapter one may think this chapter could have perhaps been the first or second chapter because Worship and Praise is the most important element in the life of all Christians.

First, we must get a clear understanding of what these two words "worship" and "praise" mean. I have broken this chapter into two separate sections so we can get a better understanding of what worship and praise mean individually, and how the two work together.

Some have said that we worship God because of who He is and we praise Him for what he has done:

- We worship God because of who He is, He is Elohim the first name used of God in the Bible to designate Him (Genesis1:1), this name means Strong and Mighty One. He is Adonai, meaning "Master," "Ruler" or "Lord" (Genesis 15:1-2). He is Jehovah, which is His personal name, meaning Redeemer and His covenant name.

Note: when we see "LORD" in the Bible, it is talking about Elohim and/or Jehovah; and when we see "Lord." the name means Adonai.

- We praise God because of the things He has done. He has delivered us out of darkness into His marvelous, wonderful light (1 Peter 2:9 NKJV); through the Light of the world which is His Son Jesus Christ. God has saved us out of the darkness of sin and death to deliver us into the light of eternity in which we shall live forever. Therefore, we are to praise God for His works in creation, His providence, His redemption and for our salvation.

Throughout the Bible worship and praise are represented as the duty of man. They understood that to fail in this duty was an act of withholding from God the glory that belongs to Him. The writer of Psalm fifty states, "Whoever offers praise glorifies Me; and to him who orders his conduct aright I will show the salvation of God" (Psalm 50:23 NKJV). Throughout the Bible we find that the holy men during biblical times did this by arousing their soul from its lazy state and by fixing their hearts upon God. They did it by meditation on God's works, recounting all His benefits to us, His love, mercy, and grace and above all, for His Son Jesus the Christ dwelling in our hearts. As Christians we are to give to God the honor and glory and gratitude we owe Him, and we must earnestly cultivate and develop a spirit and habit of worship and praise.

"WORSHIP"

In most churches, true worship is neglected because true worship is not understood. We must distinguish between the acts of worship in our worship services and learn to worship with a heart of worship. Christians must learn how to worship God so we can participate in the actual act of worship. Our worship service is often the place where most people are likely to learn the basis of worship, and it is here where we as mature and seasoned Christians should lead by example.

Worship it is the number one inherent attribute of every human, because we were all created to worship. We find individuals, groups, and nations worshiping from Genesis to Revelations. In Genesis Cain and Abel both brought offerings to God the Father (Genesis 4:3-6 KJV), and in Revelations chapter four the Bible tells us that the twenty-four elders fell down and worshiped before God's throne (Revelations 4:10 NKJV).

In a true worship experience the believers should examine and prepare themselves in light of meeting with God, because as a Christian we are expected to know that God can do for us that which only God can do. Through worship a Christian can take exclusive possession of the power and person of the Lord Jesus Christ for our lives.

The Meaning of Worship

In the Old Testament, we find the Hebrew word for worship is shaw-khaw, meaning to depress, bow down, prostrate as in Exodus 4:31 (KJV) which states, "they bowed their heads and worshipped." These words are found over ninety times in the Old Testament. Also, in the Old Testament worship is the expressing or having a respectful attitude of mind or body or both, combined with other forms of religious adoration, obedience, and service.

However, in the New Testament we find the Greek word proskuneo which is translated as worship. This word means to fall down before or bow down before. Worship is a state of spirit (an attitude), it's an internal, individual action that could and should be done all the time in our lives, regardless of place or situation. Jesus stated, "... the time is coming when it will no longer matter whether you worship the Father on this mountain or in Jerusalem" (John 4:21 NLT). This means that Christians are to worship 365 days a year, 24 hours a day. When Christians gather together in worship, it should still be an emphasis on the individual worshiping the Lord. In the congregation, all participants must know that they are worshiping a Holy God fully individually.

The Object of Worship

Throughout the Bible it is God the Father, the maker and creator of the universe, who is to be the object of our worship. The Bible states that

His whole creation praises Him, from the angels in heaven to the lower existences on the earth and that are under the earth (Revelation 5:13 BLB). John also stated that the 24 elders in the new heaven affirm this about God, by saying, "You are worthy, O Lord, To receive glory and honor and power; For You created all things, And by Your will they exist and were created" (Revelation 4:11 NKJV).

We found that the nature of worship - communion, adoration, and gratitude was seen to be the moving force behind Cain and Abel as early as in Genesis four, which states: "In the course of time Cain brought some of the fruits of the soil as an offering to the Lord. And Abel also brought an offering—fat portions from some of the firstborn of his flock. The Lord looked with favor on Abel and his offering," (Genesis 4:3-4 NIV). We find that in Genesis chapter eight Noah built an altar unto God to worship Him, and Abraham also built an altar to worship God in Genesis chapter twelve.

In the Old Testament, Moses pointed the children of Israel to Jehovah-Elohim (Yahweh). The Bible states:

- "You shall fear the LORD your God and serve Him, and shall take oaths in His name" (Deuteronomy 6:13 NKJV).

- "And now, Israel, what does the LORD your God require of you, but to fear the LORD your God, to walk in all his ways, to love him, to serve the LORD your God with all your heart and with all your soul," (Deuteronomy 10:12 ESV).

- "You shall fear the LORD your God; you shall serve Him, and to Him you shall hold fast, and take oaths in His name" (Deuteronomy 10:20 NKJV).

In the New Testament, the Apostles Barnabas, Peter, Paul and John also point out to people that God/Jesus is the only person to be worshiped, and not men! The Bible tells us:

- (The Apostles Barnabas and Paul) "Men, why are you doing these things? We also are men, of like nature with you, and we bring you good news, that you should turn from these vain things to a living God, who made the heaven and the earth and the sea and all that is in them" (Acts 14:15 ESV).

- (The Apostle Peter) "But Peter made him get up. "Stand up," he said, "I am only a man myself" (Acts 10:26 NIV).

- (The Apostle Paul) "Do not let anyone who delights in false humility and the worship of angels disqualify you. Such a person also goes into great detail about what they have seen; they are puffed up with idle notions by their unspiritual mind" (Colossians 2:18 NIV).

- (The Apostle John) At this I fell at his feet to worship him. But he said: "Do not do that! I am a fellow servant with you and your brothers who rely on the testimony of Jesus. Worship God! For the testimony of Jesus is the spirit of prophecy" (Revelation 19:10 BSB).

- (The Apostle John) "And I, John, am the one hearing and seeing these things. And when I heard and saw, I fell down to worship before the feet of the angel showing these things me" (Revelation 22:8 BLB).

And we also find in the Gospels that Jesus said to Satan; "Away from me, Satan! For it is written: 'Worship the Lord your God, and serve him only'" (Matthew 4:10; Luke 4:8 NIV).

The Method of Worship

With true worship, it must not and should not just be a repetition of a religious ritual time and time again. A particular song, a prayer, or just reading a particular scripture may lose its effectiveness when overused. We must keep our worship worthy of the Lord.

With the method, or the way, we worship, it all begins with our preparation. When we come before the Lord, our hearts and spirits should be focused on God/Jesus. We must prepare ourselves because focus is essential to worship. During our preparation, we must all examine ourselves because sincere worship begins in our hearts. As we examine our own hearts before the Lord, we may well see ourselves as we are and this will help us to line ourselves up to worship in spirit and in truth.

As we look through the Bible we find several worship experiences in which people examined themselves before worshiping God. The Bible states:

- When Isaiah was worshiping in the Temple and saw the holiness of God he cried out, "Woe is me, for I am undone! Because I am a man of unclean lips . . ." (Isaiah 6:5 NKJV).

- In the book of Exodus, we have the encounter between God and Moses at the burning bush. After speaking with God and receiving a revelation of God's holiness, Moses examined himself. Moses cried out, "Who am I that I should go to Pharaoh" (Exodus 3:11 KJV)? Moses saw his own uselessness.

- The Apostle Paul tells us we should examine ourselves before going to the communion table. Paul stated: "But let a man examine himself, and in this manner let him eat of the bread, and let him drink of the cup" (1 Corinthians 11:28 BLB). When believers participate in the Lord's Supper, all understand that it is a time when our hearts should be in true worship and praise, because it is a time of rendering unto God the glory and adoration due to Him.

We also find we should worship with an expectation. As a children of God, we should have a level of expectation when we come before the Father, because our human spirit naturally worships. Expectation is a very important key element of our faith, and we all need faith in our worship experience. The Bible states:

- "And without faith it is impossible to please God, because anyone who comes to him must believe that he exists and that he rewards those who earnestly seek him (Hebrews 11:6 NIV).

Next worship is an active form of human activity. We all know that a person cannot participate in a game unless they play in the game (standing on the sidelines differs from participating). Therefore, if a person doesn't purposely participate in worship, they cannot worship in the presence of a Holy God. Here are some ways we participate in worship:

- In our giving – Tithes and Offering: "Will a man rob God? Yet you have robbed Me! But you say, 'In what way have we robbed You?' In tithes and offerings" (Malachi 3:8 NKJV). Jesus said: "Give to Caesar what is Caesar's, and to God what is God's" (Mark 12:17; Luke 20:25 BLB).

- Sunday School – As iron sharpens iron, So one man sharpens another (Proverbs 27:17 NASB).

- Bible Study – The word of God states, "Study to show thyself approved unto God, a workman that needeth not to be ashamed, rightly dividing the word of truth" (2 Timothy 2:15 KJV).

- Quiet time – True worship involves quietness, meditation and thinking. A person receives understanding only by putting forth mental effort. This is filled with reflection that produces a spiritually effective life.

With the methods we use to worship, understand that it is all about setting or creating an atmosphere to worship a Holy God. From our preparation, to expectation, to participation, it is all about worshiping Him in line with His Word.

Worship that is Pleasing to God

Our worship must also involve our total being as we express our worship and praise to God and Jesus the Son. This type of praise and worship involves our total spirit, soul, and body.

We find throughout the Bible that the worship that is pleasing to God is the worship given in how He has instructed it. In Genesis chapter four and in chapter eight, Abel and Noah understood and followed God's instruction for pleasing and acceptable worship. The Bible tells us:

- "And Abel also brought an offering—fat portions from some of the firstborn of his flock. The LORD looked with favor on Abel and his offering" (Genesis 4:4 NIV).

- "Then Noah built an altar to the LORD and, taking some of all the clean animals and clean birds, he sacrificed burnt offerings on it. The LORD smelled the pleasing aroma and said in his heart: "Never again will I curse the ground because of man, even though every inclination of his heart is evil from childhood. And never again will I destroy all living creatures, as I have done" (Genesis 8:20-21 NIV).

One of the first things the Bible teaches is that we must worship God/Jesus in and through the Spirit. In the book of John, we find Jesus speaking to a Samaritan woman at a well, He said "Yet a time is coming and has now come when the true worshipers will worship the Father in spirit and truth, for they are the kind of worshipers the Father seeks" (John 4:23 NIV). This means we must worship God with our "spirit of man," the part of us that was made alive at our conversion. The spirit of man is our God awareness; it's the part of man in which we can fellowship with God; this is where life is given and where the Spirit of God lives. The Scriptures tells us that God "forms the spirit of man within him" (Zechariah 12:1 NKJV).

We must also worship God with our souls. Our souls are what we call our personhood; it's the whole person as dependent upon God for life's physical, emotional, and spiritual needs. The soul is where we make the majority of our decisions. It is the part of man where intellect comes in; here man can think and reason. This means we must also worship God with our minds. The Apostle Paul tells the church at Philippi that all believers should have the mind of Christ Jesus (Philippians 2:5 KJV), which is also called a renewed mind (Romans 12:2 BLB). Understand that the will/mind is a part of the human personality that must be involved in worship because pleasing and acceptable worship is an act of our will which starts in our minds.

This worship in the New Testament is translated from the Greek word "latreuo" which means to render religious service that can only occur when we exercise our wills, which have been surrendered to the will of God.

Next, we must worship God with our rededicated bodies. The Apostle Paul called the church in Rome to offer their bodies as living sacrifices, holy and pleasing to God; it is a spiritual act of worship (Romans 12:1 NIV).

God wants our bodies surrendered to Him so He can live and work through us. We find these physical acts of worship in the Bible include:

- Kneeling – "Therefore God exalted him to the highest place and gave him the name that is above every name, that at the name of Jesus every knee should bow, in heaven and on earth and under the earth" (Philippians 2:9-10 NIV).

- Bowing the head – "Is this the kind of fast I have chosen, only a day for a man to humble himself? Is it only for bowing one's head like a reed and for lying on sackcloth and ashes? Is that what you call a fast, a day acceptable to the LORD" (Isaiah 58:5 NIV)?

- Raising hands – "Because thy lovingkindness is better than life, my lips shall praise thee. Thus will I bless thee while I live: I will lift up my hands in thy name" (Psalm 63:3-4 KJV).

- Dancing – "Let them praise His name with the dance; Let them sing praises to Him with the timbrel and harp" (Psalm 149:3 NKJV).

NOTE: See the Method of Praise in the Praise section (page 140).

The Command to Worship

When we look at the Ten Commandments, one of the first things we find is that the first four commandments pertain to God the Father and how we are to relate to Him. As we look at Exodus chapter twenty we find:

"And God spoke all these words: "I am the LORD your God, who brought you out of Egypt, out of the land of slavery. "You shall have no other gods before me. "You shall not make for yourself an idol in the form of anything in heaven above or on the earth beneath or in the waters below. You shall not bow down to them or worship them; for I, the LORD your God, am a jealous God, punishing the children for the sin of the fathers to the third and fourth generation of those who hate me, but showing love to a thousand generations of those who love me and keep my commandments. "You shall not misuse the name of the LORD your God, for the LORD will not hold anyone guiltless who misuses his name. "Remember the Sabbath day by keeping it holy" (Exodus 20:1-8 NIV).

Let's look at what the Lord said to Moses on three different occasions; the first time it was verbal, the second was written with His finger, and the third time God commanded Moses to write them on stone tables for the children of Israel.

- Verse 2 – the Lord points out to the children of Israel, it was Him that saved them: "I am the LORD your God, who brought you out of Egypt, out of the land of slavery." And it is also God alone that saves man today from the bondage of sin.

- Verse 3 – the Lord God makes the command plain and clear: "You shall have no other gods before me" (also in Deuteronomy 5:7 NLT).

- Verse 4 – the Lord points out that He is a jealous God and He will punish anyone who bows down and worships any false gods.

- Verse 7 – the Lord prohibits the use of his name that takes away from His character, His works or His Holiness. We should use His name only in worship and praise.

- Verse 8 – verse eight takes us back to chapter two, "What does Jesus want most from me," where we learned that God wants a personal relationship with each of us. He wants us to rest and take the time to fellowship with him in holiness.

In the Gospels of Matthew and Luke, Jesus said to Satan; For it is written or it is commanded to worship the Lord your God, and serve him only (Matthew 4:10; Luke 4:8 NIV).

"Worship the Lord." This is more than a good idea. It is a command. God wants you and me to worship him! And he deserves it! So, we should give Him the worship he deserves!

"PRAISE"

When we consider the reasons we should praise God, we find a list of His attributes such as His holiness, His love, His mercy and grace, His faithfulness, His sovereignty, and so much more. We also praise God for His wonderful works in creation, His glorious acts of every kind, His providence, His redemption, and for all the other benefits we have received. When we praise God, we are showing Him we are surrendering our allegiance to Him and we are giving credit and honor to whom it's due.

The Meaning of Praise

First what is praise? Praise comes from a Latin word meaning "value" or "price." To give praise to God is to proclaim His merit or worth. Many terms are used to express this in the Bible which include: "glory," "magnify," "blessing," "thanksgiving," and "hallelujah," which is the name translated from the Hebrew which means "Praise the Lord."

The Hebrew name of the book of Psalms is "Praises," which comes from the same root as "hallelujah." In the Psalms we find that Psalm 113 through Psalm 118 have been specifically designated as "Hallel" Psalms ("praise").

We also have the patriarch Jacob's wife Leah naming one of his sons "Praise." The Bible tells us that after she had conceived for the fourth time, and when she gave birth to a son she said: "This time I will praise the LORD." So she named her son Judah" (Genesis 29:35 NIV), which in Hebrew means "praise" or "to praise."

The Object of Praise

With the object of our praise, it is God/Jesus who receives first place in our lives. However, sometimes man may receive praise. He may receive it from God or even his fellow man' depending upon the grounds and motives that lie behind it. In these cases, Jesus and Paul warn us about the attitude of looking for the praise of men for ourselves like the Pharisees. The Apostle John said, "for they loved praise from men more than praise from God" (John 12:43 KJV). This is itself a condemnation. There is a praise that is an automatic respect of the soul to righteousness. This is seen in Christian service to others. We find in this case Paul telling the Church at Corinth, "And we are sending along with him the brother who is praised by all the churches for his service to the gospel" (2 Corinthians 8:18 NIV). This praise can only come from holy living and an attitude of worship and praise.

In the Old and New Testaments, it is God the Father that is the object of our praise. The Bible states that His whole creation praises Him, from the angels in heaven to the lowest existing form in or on the earth and also the lowest under the earth (Revelation 5:13 KJV).

However, it is the praises offered by man to God that bring Him glory and honor. We also find in Scripture it is the duty of man to praise God and render our worship to Him only. This is the adoration we give to God and to the Lamb (Jesus), which is inspired by a sense of their worthiness to be worshiped and adored. The Apostle John wrote in Revelation:

- "Worthy are You, our Lord and our God, to receive glory and honor and power; for You created all things, and because of Your will they existed, and were created" (Revelation 4:11 NASB).

- In a loud voice they sang: "Worthy is the Lamb having been slain, to receive the power and riches and wisdom and strength and honor and glory and blessing" (Revelation 5:12 BLB)!

Sometimes we praise God for His inherent qualities:

For His "Holiness"

- "And one cried unto another, and said, Holy, holy, holy, is the LORD of hosts: the whole earth is full of his glory" (Isaiah 6:3 KJV).

- "Exalt the LORD our God, and worship at his holy hill; for the LORD our God is holy" (Psalm 99:9 KJV).

- "Each of the four living creatures had six wings and was covered with eyes all around, even under its wings. Day and night they never stop saying: "'Holy, holy, holy is the Lord God Almighty,' who was, and is, and is to come" (Revelation 4:8 NIV).

For His "Majesty"

- "Praise the LORD, my soul. LORD my God, you are very great; you are clothed with splendor and majesty" (Psalm 104:1 NIV).

- "They lift up their voices, they sing for joy; over the majesty of the LORD they shout from the west" (Isaiah 24:14 ESV).

For His "Glory"

- "We pray this so that the name of our Lord Jesus may be glorified in you, and you in him, according to the grace of our God and the Lord Jesus Christ" (2 Thessalonians 1:12 NIV).

- "Through him you believe in God, who raised him from the dead and glorified him, and so your faith and hope are in God" (1 Peter 1:21 NIV).

Sometimes we praise God for His communicable attribute (the inherent characteristic of His nature):

For His "Love"

- "Praise the LORD! Give thanks to the LORD, for he is good! His faithful love endures forever" (Psalm 106:1 NLT).

- "For his unfailing love for us is powerful; the LORD's faithfulness endures forever. Praise the LORD" (Psalm 117:2 NLT).

For His "Mercy"

- "Praise be to the LORD, for he has heard my cry for mercy" (Psalm 28:6 NIV).

- Paul tells us, "But God, being rich in mercy, because of His great love with which He loved us" (Ephesians 2:4 BLB).

For His "Grace"

- "Great is the LORD and most worthy of praise; his greatness no one can fathom" (Psalm 145:3 NIV).

- Paul states, "For by grace you are saved through faith, and this not of yourselves; it is the gift of God" (Ephesians 2:8 BLB).

Again, we praise God mostly for His works in creation, providence, and for our redemption. From Genesis to Revelation we find people giving God praise, particularly in the book of Psalms where it is God alone that loves us and is most worthy of our praise, blessing and thanksgiving. Peter said it best when he said: "Praise be to the God and Father of our Lord Jesus Christ! In his great mercy, he has given us new birth into a living hope through the resurrection of Jesus Christ from the dead" (1 Peter 1:3 NIV).

The Method of Praise

Praise should be an emotional and intellectual choice of our will and a moral response to God. Worship is a spirit-to-spirit participation with a living God, based on the prompting of the Holy Spirit, which results in the exaltation of giving God/Jesus glory.

Our praise is also personal. Praise is not just an intellectual process; it involves more than knowledge and fact about God. Praise should stir the emotions in each of us so that it results in physical and spiritual activity.

As we look through the Bible we find various forms and method of praise, such as dancing, singing, and the playing of instruments. The Bible tells us:

With our Mouths:

- "With my mouth I will greatly extol the LORD; in the great throng I will praise him" (Psalm 109:30 NIV).

- "Praise God in the great congregation; praise the LORD in the assembly . . ." (Psalm 68:26 NIV).

- "Blessed be the LORD, the God of Israel, from everlasting to everlasting! And let all the people say, "Amen!" Praise the LORD" (Psalm 106:48 ESV).

- "My mouth will speak the praise of the LORD, and let all flesh bless his holy name forever and ever" (Psalm 145:21 ESV).

- "Through Jesus, therefore, let us continually offer to God a sacrifice of praise, the fruit of lips that confess His name" (Hebrews 13:15 BSB).

Note: some words are created or made for the children of God such as the word, "hallelujah!" This word comes from two compound Hebrew words, "hallal" and "jah." The first word, "hallal," means "to praise," and the word "jah" is the word for God, this gives us the word Jehovah. This word simply means "praise be to God" or "praise the Lord."[23]

With our Hands:

- "I will praise you as long as I live, and in your name I will lift up my hands" (Psalm 63:4 NIV).

- "Lift up your hands in the sanctuary and praise the LORD" (Psalm 134:2 NIV).

- "I lift up my hands to Your commandments, which I love, and I meditate on Your statutes" (Psalm 119:48 BSB).

With our Dance:

- David's leaping and dancing before the Lord was expressive of joy and praise to God. David's dancing is described in 2 Samuel 6.

- "Then David danced before the LORD with all his might; and David was wearing a linen ephod" (2 Samuel 6:14 NKJV).

With Instruments:

- "and it was the duty of the trumpeters and singers to make themselves heard in unison in praise and thanksgiving to the LORD, and when the song was raised, with trumpets and cymbals and other musical instruments, in praise to the LORD, "For he is good, for his steadfast love endures forever," the house, the house of the LORD, was filled with a cloud" (2 Chronicles 5:13 ESV).

- "Praise the LORD with the harp; Make melody to Him with an instrument of ten strings" (Psalm 33:2 NKJV).

- "Then David spoke to the leaders of the Levites to appoint their brethren to be the singers accompanied by instruments of music, stringed instruments, harps, and cymbals, by raising the voice with resounding joy" (1 Chronicles 15:16 NKJV).

- "When the builders laid the foundation of the temple of the LORD, the priests in their vestments and with trumpets, and the Levites (the sons of Asaph) with cymbals, took their places to praise the LORD, as prescribed by David king of Israel" (Ezra 3:10 NIV).

- "When Nehemiah dedicated of the Wall of Jerusalem, the Bible tells us they used instruments in the celebration: "Now at the dedication of the wall of Jerusalem they sought out the Levites in all their places, to bring them to Jerusalem to celebrate the dedication with gladness, both with thanksgivings and singing, with cymbals and stringed instruments and harps" (Nehemiah 12:27 NKJV).

With our Singing:

- "Sing praises to the LORD, O you his saints, and give thanks to his holy name" (Psalm 30:4 ESV).

- "Sing joyfully to the LORD, you righteous; it is fitting for the upright to praise him (Psalm 33:1 NIV).

- "He put a new song in my mouth, a song of praise to our God. Many will see and fear, and put their trust in the LORD" (Psalm 40:3 ESV).

- "Sing to God! Sing praises to His name. Exalt Him who rides on the clouds—His name is the LORD—and rejoice before Him" (Psalm 68:4 BSB).

- "I will be glad and rejoice in you; I will sing the praises of your name, O Most High" (Psalm 9:2 NIV).

- "I will sing to the LORD all my life; I will sing praise to my God as long as I live" (Psalm 104:33 NIV).

- "Praise the LORD! Sing to the LORD a new song, And His praise in the assembly of saints" (Psalm 149:1 NKJV).

- "Speak to one another with psalms, hymns and spiritual songs. Sing and make music in your heart to the Lord, always giving thanks to God the Father for everything, in the name of our Lord Jesus Christ" (Ephesians 5:19-20 NIV).

Therefore, whatever the method of praise we may use, it must come from a heart and a spirit of worship and praise.

Praise that is Pleasing to God

While the Bible is filled with individual and groups offering praise to God, there are also occasional warnings about the quality of this praise. Christian praise should originate in the hearts of all believers; it's an inward emotion, a gladness and rejoicing of the heart, its music in one's soul and spirit. Christian praise should never be an outward show, as seen in Matthew chapter fifteen which Jesus states, "These people honor me with their lips, but their hearts are far from me" (Matthew 15:8 NIV).

The Bible also shows us the difference between true praise and false praise to God; the Lord said to Isaiah, "These people draw near to Me with their mouths and honor Me with their lips, but their hearts are far from Me. Their worship of Me is but rules taught by men" (Isaiah 29:13 BSB).

When we as individuals offer praise to God, it should come from a lifestyle of praise and worship and not as a religious duty or obligation. God said to Amos, "I hate, I despise your feast days, And I do not savor your sacred assemblies. Though you offer Me burnt offerings and your grain offerings, I will not accept them, Nor will I regard your fattened peace offerings. Take away from Me the noise of your songs, For I will not hear the melody of your stringed instruments. But let justice run down like water, And righteousness like a mighty stream." (Amos 5:21-24 NKJV)!

Understand that a corrupt heart in praise and worship is despised by the Lord. Our praise and worship is all about having the right heart (attitude).

Now with group or corporate praise offering to God, it should be in an orderly manner. The Apostle Paul told the Corinthian church that everything should be done in a fitting and orderly way in first Corinthians, chapter fourteen (14:40 KJV). God expects us to praise Him in an expression of reverence and commitment to Him. However, He wants even more. God also expects us to be obedient to Him and act justly towards each other by showing love and compassion to others. The best way to sum up the worship and praise that's pleasing to God is in His Word, and we find it in the Old and New Testaments. We find:

- "Hear, O Israel: The Lord our God, the Lord is one! You shall love the Lord your God with all your heart, with all your soul, and with all your strength" (Deuteronomy 6:4-5 NKJV).

- "And now, Israel, what does the LORD your God require of you, but to fear the LORD your God, to walk in all His ways and love Him, and to serve the LORD your God with all your heart and with all your soul," (Deuteronomy 10:12 NASB).

- Jesus replied, "' You shall love the Lord your God with all your heart, and with all your soul, and with all your mind" (Matthew 22:37 BLB).

The Command to Praise

The writer of Psalm 148 tells us that all of creation is commanded to give praise to God:

"Praise the LORD. Praise the LORD from the heavens; praise him in the heights above. Praise him, all his angels, praise him, all his heavenly hosts. Praise him, sun and moon, praise him, all you shining stars. Praise him, you highest heavens and you waters above the skies. Let them praise the name of the LORD, for he commanded and they were created. He set them in place forever and ever; he gave a decree that will never pass away. Praise the LORD from the earth, you great sea creatures and all ocean depths, lightning and hail, snow and clouds, stormy winds that do his bidding, you mountains and all hills, fruit trees and all cedars, wild animals and all cattle, small creatures and flying birds" (Psalm 148:1-10 NIV).

The Bible also tells us that when Jesus was entering Jerusalem on Palm Sunday a great crowd gathered and offered Him their praises. While the Pharisees wanted Him to rebuke the people, Jesus answered: "I tell you that if these should keep silent, the stones would immediately cry out" (Luke 19:40 NKJV).

The Lord God told the children of Israel, "Hear, O Israel: The Lord our God, the Lord is one! You shall love the Lord your God with all your heart, with all your soul, and with all your strength. "And these words which I command you today shall be in your heart" (Deuteronomy 6:4-6 NKJV).

Therefore, praise is what we should do, and we should express our thanksgiving and love unto the Lord.

Next, we must learn to worship and praise God through our pain and suffering. In every person's life, we will all have someone close to us die, we will all experience sickness, and we all will suffer disappointment at some point. During these times, we must worship and praise God all the more.

The Bible tells us that Job lost practically everything he had. It states that the Sabeans attacked and carried off his seven thousand sheep, five hundred yoke of oxen and five hundred donkeys. All but four of his servants were killed. The Chaldeans formed three raiding parties and swept down on his three thousand camels and carried them off. And a mighty wind struck the corners of the house where his seven sons and three daughters were, and it collapsed on them, killing them all. The Bible states that Job got up and tore his robe and shaved his head. Then he fell to the ground and worshiped. Then he said, "Naked I came from my mother's womb, And naked I shall return there. The LORD gave and the LORD has taken away. Blessed be the name of the LORD" (Job 1:21 NASB).

We also find in the Bible that Paul and Silas were stripped and beaten, then put into prison. And we are told that around midnight they prayed and sang hymns to the Lord. Here we find they worshiped and praised God through their pain and suffering. We can read about it in the book of Acts chapter sixteen, starting at the sixteenth verse.

In conclusion, to praise and worship, we must understand the reasons, the purpose, and the benefits for our praise and worship. First, it's for the glory of God the Father and the honoring of our Lord and Savior Jesus Christ. Second, praise and worship will and can change the atmosphere and bring our spirit into a place of true peace, the peace that passes all understanding, the peace that can only come from God. Third, worship and praise will also bring us into a oneness with God the Father. When we learn the joy and benefits of worship and praise, our lives will never be the same.

However, we also understand that for some Christians praise and worship is something they must learn, because some people in today's churches have never experienced a genuine praise and worship (oneness through the Holy Spirit to God/Jesus). We all must understand that praise and worship is not only for God, but it also affects the worshiper. This may mean there are many people in our churches today missing out on an important dimension of the Christian life.

We were created to worship! We praise God for saving us out of the darkness of sin and death, and He has delivered us into the light of eternity. Therefore, we must follow Paul as he followed Christ and let the word of God/Jesus dwell in us richly as we teach and admonish one another with all wisdom, singing of psalms, hymns and spiritual songs with gratitude in our hearts to God (Colossians 3:16 BSB).

PRAYER:

> Lord God, my hallelujah belongs to you. We worship and praise you because you are the one and only true and living God; You alone are worthy of praise, glory and honor. In Jesus' name – AMEN

Reflection Time:

1. Why is Praise and Worship the most important element in the life of all Christians?

   _____

   _____

   _____

   _____

   _____

   _____

   _____

2. We worship God because of?

   _____

   _____

   _____

   _____

   _____

   _____

3. We praise God because of?

   _____

   _____

   _____

   _____

   _____

   _____

4. What does the word "hallelujah" mean?

   _____

   _____

   _____

   _____

   _____

   _____

5. The purpose and benefits for our praise and worship are:
   • First, it's for _____

   _____

   _____

   • Second, praise and worship _____

   _____

   _____

   • Third, worship and praise will _____

   _____

   _____

6. With the method or the way, we worship, it all begins with our

   _____

   _____

   _____.

7. How can you apply what you've learned in this chapter to your personal life?

   _____

   _____

   _____

   _____

   _____

   _____

   _____

   _____

8. What step will you commit to take to create a better worship and praise atmosphere for yourself?

   _____

   _____

   _____

   _____

   _____

   _____

   _____

   _____

9. Who will be the person that will hold you accountable in this area?

_____

_____

_____

_____

_____

_____

 "You are worthy, O Lord, To receive glory and honor and power; For You created all things, And by Your will they exist and were created" (Revelation 4:11 NKJV).

Chapter Ten

"The Importance of the Church"

"Do not think that I have come to abolish the Law or the Prophets; I have not come to abolish them but to fulfill them. For truly I tell you, until heaven and earth disappear, not the smallest letter, not the least stroke of a pen, will by any means disappear from the Law until everything is accomplished. Therefore, anyone who sets aside one of the least of these commands and teaches others accordingly will be called least in the kingdom of heaven, but whoever practices and teaches these commands will be called great in the kingdom of heaven" (Matthew 5:17-19 NIV).

When I was growing up, the Church was one of the most important things and places in the lives of my family and the people in my neighborhood. However, most of the world today does not hold the church in high regards and honor.

We should understand that the church is the third institution set-up by God himself. The first is marriage and family: Genesis 2:24 (ESV) says, "Therefore a man shall leave his father and his mother and hold fast to his wife, and they shall become one flesh." The second institution is government: Romans 13:1 (NASB) state, "Every person is to be subject to the governing authorities. For there is no authority except from God, and those which exist are established by God." And the third institution is the

Church; in the book Matthew, we are told that Jesus was going to build His church (Matthew 16:18 KJV). We are also told that Jesus purchased that church with His blood (Acts 20:28 BSB), and that He is the head of the Church (Ephesians 1:22-23 BLB).

Therefore, as a Christian we must uphold all three of God's divine institutions in high regards and honor because He rules in all three.

What the Church is NOT!

The church is not your Christian radio station; it is not a Christian television program. It is not sitting in front of your computer, or your iPad or iPhone. These things are forms of viewing or listening to Christianity without being participants in the reality of the life of the Church. The development of Christian media, Christian personalities, and Christian music have become a substitute for the Church for a number of believers today.

Church is not all about any single person. It's not about the pastor, and it's not about the members. It's not about the worship leader or the music, and church isn't even all about you or any other individual . . . "It's about Jesus Christ!"

The Church is not the place for social status. The Church is not the place for personal networking. The Church is not for your entertainment or to make you feel good. The Church is not a place where you will find perfect people. However, you can find some broken and redeemed people.

What is the Church?

The dictionary says that the church is a building used for public Christian worship; place of worship, house of God, house of worship; cathedral, abbey, chapel, basilica; megachurch; synagogue, mosque. Most people today would agree with the dictionary and say that the church is a building. However, this is not the biblical definition of the Church. The word "Church" comes from the Greek word *"ekklesia"* which means "an assembly" or "called-out ones." The early Church was wherever the meeting took place; believers thrived on fellowship with other believers and the teaching of God's Word. Acts 2:46 (NIV) states, "Every day they continued to meet together in the temple courts. They broke bread in their homes and ate together with glad and sincere hearts." Also, the early Church never called a building the church; they called the body of believers the Church. The Apostle Paul said in Romans 16:3-5 (BLB), "Greet Prisca and Aquila, my fellow workers in Christ Jesus— who have lain down their neck for my life, whom not only I thank, but also all the churches of the Gentiles— and the church at their house." Therefore, the church is a body of believers.

The Church is also the body of Christ; with Jesus Christ as the head. Ephesians 1:22-23 (NIV) states, "And God placed all things under his feet and appointed him to be head over everything for the church, which is his body, the fullness of him who fills everything in every way."

Therefore, this means that when we came to salvation, we were placed by the Holy Spirit into the body of Jesus Christ. This is known as the Universal Church. The Universal Church is everyone that believers in Jesus Christ as Lord and Savior throughout the world. The local church is a place or location where a particular group of Christians worship on a regular basis along with non-believers.

It is important that every believer attend a local church because that is where biblical teaching, serving, and spiritual growth should take place. And the local church is also known as a "family."

The Reasons some People Don't Join the Church!

The reasons some people don't join the Church is that some people never truly understand that joining the Church is an act of surrender, obedience, accountability, and an act of faith.

Let's start with the area of surrender. To become a Christian, we must all give total control of our lives to Jesus. This means our time, our energy, and our resources. Most people don't join the Church because they don't understand that everyone is a "stewards." We are all stewards of the things God has entrusted unto us, and we own "nothing." The Bible tells us in the book of Luke the Parable of the Dishonest Manager; the owner said to the manager, "What is this I hear about you? Give an account of your stewardship, for you can no longer be steward" (Luke 16:2 NKJV). The Apostle Paul said, "I became a minister according to the stewardship from God that was given to me for you, to make the word of God fully known" (Colossians 1:25 ESV). Our time, energy, and resources all belong to the Lord Jesus Christ.

There are also some people that will not submit to church leadership or church doctrines. These individuals do not understand that change by doing so to submitting is an act of surrender and obedience. In Romans 13:1 (NIV) state, "Let everyone be subject to the governing authorities, for there is no authority except that which God has established. The authorities that exist have been established by God." Titus 3:1 (NIV) state, "Remind the people to be subject to rulers and authorities, to be obedient, to be ready to do whatever is good." And, Hebrews 13:17 (NIV) tells us, "Have confidence in your leaders and submit to their authority, because they keep watch over you as those who must give an account. Do this so that their work will be a joy, not a burden, for that would be of no benefit to you." Therefore, the Bible commands the Christian to surrender and submit.

The second area why some people don't join the Church is accountability. Most people do not want to be held accountable for their life style or their actions. However, Romans 3:19 (NIV) tells us: "Now we know that whatever the Law says, it says to those who are under the Law, so that every mouth may be silenced and the whole world held accountable to God."

The third area why some people don't join the Church is fear. Fear may very well be the reason for not being able to surrender. The unwillingness for obedience could be from lack of faith. The Church may very well be the place to teach and help you overcome fear. In 1 John 4:18 (NIV) states, "There is no fear in love. But perfect love drives out fear, because fear has to do with punishment. The one who fears is not made perfect in love." And Revelation 12:11 (NKJV) says, "And they overcame him by the blood of the Lamb and by the word of their testimony . . ."

The fourth reason why some people don't join the Church is because the church does not have a particular ministry that fits them personally (single, youth, or children's ministry). There is nothing wrong with wanting to have these ministries in the church. One of the reasons why the church may not have a particular ministry is because God wants you to start it. Second Thessalonians 2:14 (NASB) states, "It was for this He called you through our gospel, that you may obtain the glory of our Lord Jesus Christ."

The fifth reason why some people don't join the Church is that most people outside the church view the Church as a group of perfect people; they think Church member are someone that has never done anything wrong. Or they may think that the church is filled with hypocrites. Both of these views are far from the truth. The truth is that "all have sinned" (Romans 3:23 BLB), and "there is no one who does good, not even one" (Romans 3:12 BSB). The problem with these two views is that the people in the Church are not the standard of the Church . . . Jesus is! He said in John 14:6 (BLB), "I am The way and The truth and The life." We are told to keep "Let us fix our eyes on Jesus, the author and perfecter of our faith" (Hebrews 12:2 BSB). Again, the Church is not a place where you will find perfect people; it the place where you find broken people and redeemed people.

The Benefits of the Church

The first benefit of the Church is that your family will instantly grow. These are the people that God has brought into your life for your spiritual benefit and blessing and for you to serve. The Church provides the opportunities for believers to learn from each other as they apply the gospel within the intimacy of relationships. The Church is a place where we can discuss and learn to apply the Scripture together. The Church is a place where we can encourage and hold each other accountable as we follow the Lord together.

1. The Church is a place where we can grow in our salvation. Remember that salvation is the process in by which God conforms the life and character of the believer into that of

Jesus through the Holy Spirit (chapter 1, understanding of our sanctification). Salvation is in three forms: instantly, positionally, and progressively:

- The first form is instantly: I AM – A New Creature; the Bible tells us, "Therefore, if anyone is in Christ, he is a new creation; old things have passed away; behold, all things have become new" (2 Corinthians 5:17 NKJV)!

- The second form of sanctification is our position in Christ Jesus. It's Positional: we have been "raised us up with Christ and seated with Him in the heavenly" (Ephesians 2:6 BSB).

- The third level is progressive: Paul tells, "I press on toward the goal to win the prize for which God has called me heavenward in Christ Jesus" (Philippians 3:14 NIV). The progressive part of our sanctification is man's responsibility and it's a command.

2. The Church is a place where we hear the truth of the Word of God. Paul tells us in Romans: How, then, can they call on the one they have not believed in? And how can they believe in the one of whom they have not heard? And how can they hear without someone preaching to them? And how can anyone preach unless they are sent? As it is written, "... How beautiful are the feet of those who bring good news" (Romans 10:15 NIV)!

- 1 Thessalonians 2:13 (NASB), "For this reason we also constantly thank God that when you received the word of God which you heard from us, you accepted it not as the word of mere men, but as what it really is, the word of God, which also is at work in you who believe."

- Ephesians 1:13 (ESV), "In him you also, when you heard the word of truth, the gospel of your salvation, and believed in him, were sealed with the promised Holy Spirit."

3. The Church is the place for each individual to publicly be baptized and give their profession of faith in Christ. Jesus told the disciples to go and make disciples, of every nations, baptizing them in the name of the Father and of the Son and of the Holy Spirit.

- Galatians 3:27 (NIV), "For all of you who were baptized into Christ have clothed yourselves with Christ."

- Acts 22:16 (NIV), "And now what are you waiting for? Get up, be baptized and wash your sins away, calling on his name."

- Romans 6:3 (NIV), "Or don't you know that all of us who were baptized into Christ Jesus were baptized into his death?"

4. The Church is where we learn how to grow as a believer. There are a lot of things you need to know about the Christian life, and Church is probably one of the most important places to start.

- 1 Peter 2:2 (NIV), "Like newborn babies, crave pure spiritual milk, so that by it you may grow up in your salvation."

- 2 Peter 3:18 (NIV), "But grow in the grace and knowledge of our Lord and Savior Jesus Christ. To him be glory both now and forever! Amen."

5. The Church is where we learn sound doctrine. Sound doctrine is important because our faith is based on the gospel message. Also, you should learn sound doctrine because what we believe affects what we do.

- Titus 2:1 (BLB), "But you, speak the things that are consistent with the sound doctrine."

- 2 Timothy 4:2-4 (NIV), "Preach the word; be prepared in season and out of season; correct, rebuke and encourage- with great patience and careful instruction. For the time will come when people will not put up with sound doctrine. Instead, to suit their own desires, they will gather around them a great number of teachers to say what their itching ears want to hear. They will turn their ears away from the truth and turn aside to myths."

- Titus 1:9 (NASB), "holding firmly the faithful word which is in accordance with the teaching, so that he will be able both to exhort in sound doctrine and to refute those who contradict it."

6. The Church is where we learn the Christian characteristic of Christ Jesus. Church is a place you can learn holiness, and how Jesus responded.

- Psalms 15:2 (NIV), "The one whose walk is blameless, who does what is righteous, who speaks the truth from their heart;"

- Philippians 2:15 (NASB), "So that you will prove yourselves to be blameless and innocent, children of God above reproach in the midst of a crooked and perverse generation, among whom you appear as lights in the world."

- Colossians 3:12 (NASB), "So, as those who have been chosen of God, holy and beloved, put on a heart of compassion, kindness, humility, gentleness and patience."

7. The Church is where we learn how to live the Christian life. It's the place where we learn what real community is all about.

- Romans 12:2 (NIV), "Do not conform to the pattern of this world, but be transformed by the renewing of your mind. Then you will be able to test and approve what God's will is—his good, pleasing and perfect will."

- Ephesians 4:32 (NKJV), "And be kind to one another, tenderhearted, forgiving one another, even as God in Christ forgave you."

- James 1:19-20 (ESV), "Know this, my beloved brothers: let every person be quick to hear, slow to speak, slow to anger; for the anger of man does not produce the righteousness of God."

8. The Church is where we learn how to love, and the meaning of genuine Love.

- 1 Corinthians 13:4-7 (NIV), "Love is patient, love is kind. It does not envy, it does not boast, it is not proud. It does not dishonor others, it is not self-seeking, it is not easily angered; it keeps no record of wrongs. Love does not delight in evil but rejoices with the truth. It always protects, always trusts, always hopes; always perseveres."

- Romans 5:8 (ESV), "But God shows his love for us in that while we were still sinners, Christ died for us."

- John 3:16 (NASB), "For God so loved the world, that He gave His only Son, so that everyone who believes in Him will not perish, but have eternal life."

9. The Church is where we learn how to serve the Lord.

  - Romans 12:11 (NIV), "Never be lacking in zeal, but keep your spiritual fervor, serving the LORD."

  - Colossians 3:23-24 (NIV), "Whatever you do, work at it with all your heart, as working for the LORD, not for human masters, since you know that you will receive an inheritance from the LORD as a reward. It is the LORD Christ you are serving."

  - Matthew 6:24 (ESV), "No one can serve two masters, for either he will hate the one and love the other, or he will be devoted to the one and despise the other. You cannot serve God and money."

10. The Church teaches us the Holiness of God, and the Church is where we learn how to set Christ like standards for our lives.

  - Luke 10:27 (NLT), "The man answered, "'You must love the LORD your God with all your heart, all your soul, all your strength, and all your mind.' And, 'Love your neighbor as yourself.'"

  - Romans 13:8-10 (ESV), "Owe no one anything, except to love each other, for the one who loves another has fulfilled the law. For the commandments, "You shall not commit adultery, You shall not murder, You shall not steal, You shall not covet," and any other commandment, are summed up in this word: "You shall love your neighbor as yourself." Love does no wrong to a neighbor; therefore, love is the fulfilling of the law."

  - Leviticus 19:2 and 1 Peter 1:16 (NIV) states, "Be holy because I, the LORD your God, am holy."

11. The Church is where we learn exercise our Gifts. The Church needs you to be there so that the body of Christ can operate in

every area. Each member of the congregation benefits from each other's spiritual gift, and that is what brings God glory.

- The Holy Spirit has given every believer at least one spiritual gift.

- The spiritual gifts are identified as: wisdom, the word of knowledge, faith, healing, miraculous powers, prophecy, distinguishing between spirits, speaking in tongues and interpretation of tongues in 1 Corinthians 12:4–11 (BSB).

- Ephesians 4:11-13 (NIV) states, "So Christ himself gave the apostles, the prophets, the evangelists, the pastors and teachers, to equip his people for works of service, so that the body of Christ may be built up until we all reach unity in the faith and in the knowledge of the Son of God and become mature, attaining to the whole measure of the fullness of Christ." These are the administration gifts for leading and teaching the Church.

12. The Church is where we could meet our spouse. Outside of making Jesus Christ the Lord of your life, picking your spouse is the second most important decision anyone will ever make. The Church is the place we can get biblical counseling and God's Holy view of marriage.

- Proverbs 18:22 (NASB), "He who finds a wife finds a good thing and obtains favor from the LORD."

- Proverbs 31:10 (BSB), "A wife of noble character, who can find? She is far more precious than rubies."

- Genesis 2:24 (NKJV), "Therefore a man shall leave his father and mother and be joined to his wife, and they shall become one flesh."

13. The Church is the place to raise our children and grandchildren. The Church is the second place in which your children can see the Christian life lived out. It is a place where they can begin to learn and grow in the Word of God.

- Proverbs 22:6 (KJV), "Train up a child in the way he should go, and when he is old, he will not depart from it".

- Ephesians 6:4 (NLT), "Fathers, do not provoke your children to anger by the way you treat them. Rather, bring them up with the discipline and instruction that comes from the Lord."

- Psalm 78:4 (NIV), "We will not hide them from their descendants; we will tell the next generation the praiseworthy deeds of the LORD, his power, and the wonders he has done."

14. The Church is where we can find an intimate circle of lifelong friends. The Church is one of the best places to find individuals that can help you grow as a Christian and hold you accountable.

- Ecclesiastes 4:9-12 (NKJV), "Two are better than one, Because they have a good reward for their labor. For if they fall, one will lift up his companion. But woe to him who is alone when he falls, For he has no one to help him up. Again, if two lie down together, they will keep warm; But how can one be warm alone? Though one may be overpowered by another, two can withstand him. And a threefold cord is not quickly broken."

- Proverbs 27:17 (NASB), "As iron sharpens iron, so one person sharpens another."

- Proverbs 12:26 (NIV), "The righteous choose their friends carefully, but the way of the wicked leads them astray."

The Importance of the Church

The Church is important because we are told -- "not forsaking the assembling together of ourselves as is the custom with some, but encouraging one another, and so much more as you see the Day drawing near" (Hebrews 10:25 BLB). So it is a command! We should understand why Paul warns us not to forsake the "assembling of ourselves together." One of the consequences of doing so could lead to our committing the unpardonable sin. Second, it is to help us and fellow believers to encourage each other so that we will not become lazy or complacent. And third, it is about other people; so, we could study and meet in small groups and share what the Holy Spirit is doing in our lives.

The Bible also tells us that we need to attend church so we can learn how to worship God and be taught His Word for our spiritual growth with other believers. Acts 2:42 (NIV) states, "They devoted themselves to the apostles' teaching and to the fellowship, to the breaking of bread and to prayer."

The second reason why the Church is important is because the church is the body of Jesus on earth. Ephesians 1:22-23 (NASB) states, "And He put all things in subjection under His feet, and gave Him as head over all things to the Church, which is His body, the fullness of Him who fills all in all."

Third, the Church is important because it is one of the ways God intends to accomplish his mission in the world. We are the hands and feet of our Lord and Savior Jesus Christ, and it is our responsibility to fulfill the Great Commission that He has given to all Christians. Matthew 28:19-20 (NIV) states, "... go and make disciples of all nations, baptizing them in the name of the Father and of the Son and of the Holy Spirit, and teaching them to obey everything I have commanded you. And surely, I am with you always, to the very end of the age." Therefore, it is the job of the Church (you and me) to take the gospel across the street, throughout our communities, our county and around the world.

The Fourth reason why the Church is important is because of the diseases all over the world; mental, physical, and spiritual. Some examples of these types if disease are Aids, cancer, heart disease, there is also adultery, violence, lust, and pride. However, we know that the ultimate disease of all times is "SIN" which has been mankind's problem from the beginning of creation. We the Church have been given the answer to their eternal problem; and the answer is Jesus Christ. It is our duty to make the proclamation of the biblical and historical person and works of Jesus Christ, with the purpose of persuading men and women all over the world to put their trust in him exclusively, as their only means of salvation. With this cure, people can rise above poverty, be freed from the bondage of sin, and their eye and hearts may be open to the truth. "We must tell people about the gospel of Jesus Christ!"

The fifth reason why the church is important is because Jesus is the Cornerstone of the Church. Peter tells us in 1 Peter 2:6 (NIV), "For in Scripture it says, "See, I lay a stone in Zion, a chosen and precious cornerstone, and the one who trusts in him will never be put to shame." Therefore, we are "living stones," building up a spiritual house to be a holy priesthood, to offer spiritual sacrifices acceptable to God through Jesus Christ (1 Peter 2:5 NIV).

The Things you should look for in choosing a Church:

What are the Elements of a Christian Church, or what should a person look for in a True Church of God? Do the church teaches and believe the following doctrine?

1. The number one thing is their doctrine – does it line-up with the Word of God?

   a. The Scriptures (the Bible), in Both the Old and New Testament are verbally inspired by God and are inerrant in the original writings. That God - The Holy Spirit wrote the Bible, with man as its instrument. Through the providence of God, the Scriptures have been preserved and are the supreme and final authority in faith and life.

      • Does the Church understand that the Bible is an amazing historical, scientific, and prophetic accuracy of universal influence and life transforming power; all which show that the Bible could only come from the hand of God?

   b. What is their doctrine of God? Do they believe that God is unique in nature, that no person, object, or idea can compare to Him? Therefore, anything we say about God must be based on His revelation of Himself to us. The reality of God is always much greater than our human minds can understand or express.

- There is only One living and true God, who is infinite in being and perfection. He is the creator of all, He the "HOLY"!

c. Their doctrine of Jesus is one of the most important questions you should ask is . . . "Who do you say Jesus is?" Jesus is the eternal Son of God; He is the Lord and Savior of the world; the second person of the Trinity (Philippians 2:5-11 NKJV). The incarnation of Jesus is that in the one person, there are two natures, a human nature and a divine nature; each in its completeness and integrity. Jesus was God in human flesh led by the Holy Spirit to provide salvation for all men (John 1:14 KJV).

- The Prophet Isaiah said, "... And His name will be called Wonderful, Counselor, Mighty God, Everlasting Father, Prince of Peace" (Isaiah 9:6 NKJV).

- The Apostle John said, "In the beginning was the Word, and the Word was with God, and the Word was God. He was with God in the beginning. Through him all things were made; without him nothing was made that has been made ... The Word became flesh and made his dwelling among us. We have seen his glory, the glory of the one and only Son, who came from the Father, full of grace and truth" (John 1:1-3, 14 NIV).

- The Apostle Thomas called Him "My Lord and my God" (John 20:28 KJV)!

- The Apostle Peter replied, "You are the Christ, the Son of the living God" (Matthew 16:16 ESV).

- Jesus said about Himself, "'I am the Alpha and the Omega,' says the Lord God, 'who is and who was and who is to come, the Almighty'" (Revelation 1:8 NIV).

- God the Father said about Jesus: "'... You are My Son; today I have begotten You"? And again: "I will be to Him a Father, And He shall be to Me a Son"? But when He again brings the firstborn into the world, He says: "Let all the angels of God worship Him." And of the angels

He says: "Who makes His angels spirits And His ministers a flame of fire." But to the Son He says: "Your throne, O God, is forever and ever; A scepter of righteousness is the scepter of Your kingdom" (Hebrews 1:5-8 NKJV).

d. What is their doctrine of the Holy Spirit? The Holy Spirit is the third person in the Trinity, very God, co-existent with the Father and the Son. The Holy Spirit was active in creation (Genesis 1:2 KJV). The Holy Spirit is the chief agent in the regeneration that baptizes the believer into the body of Christ, by His indwelling of an individual. The Holy Spirit convicts us of sin, and is a comforter of the believer (Luke 12:12; Romans 15:13 NKJV).

e. What is their doctrine of Man? Man is the direct creation of God – body, soul, and spirit. Therefore man is not the result of evolution but is made in the image of God. Because of this divine action, man has both a material and a spiritual nature. This means man has a spirit and soul and body (1 Thessalonians 5:23; Malachi 2:15; Matthew 10:28 KJV).

f. What is their doctrine of Satan? In Christianity, the Devil or Satan's original name is Lucifer. He was an angel who rebelled against God, and he has been condemned to the lake of fire and brimstone (Revelation 19:20 KJV). He is described as hating all humanity, spreading lies and deceit among the world. Satan also accuses Christians before God (Job 1:7-12; 2:3-6; Revelation 12:9-10 KJV).

g. What is their doctrine of Angels? The angels are represented throughout the Bible as a body of spiritual beings. They are intermediaries between God and men. An angle was created by God to be Holy messengers, who delivers God's message of instructions, warnings, or hope (Luke 2:8-11 NIV). They are mighty warriors (Daniel 10:13; Revelation 12:7-9 KJV); they are ministering spirits sent to serve those who will inherit salvation (Hebrews 1:14 NKJV).

h. What is their doctrine of Sin? Sin is the universal human condition of the broken relationship with God involving thereby missing the mark, to overstep a forbidden line, and breaking God's instructions, there by falling short of His intention for human life (Romans 3:23 KJV). Sin is doing your will, and not doing the will of God. Sin may be thought of as anything that robs God of His glory and man of his good. Sin is also a lack of conformity to the moral law of God by act, disposition (attitude) or condition of mind.

i. What is their doctrine of Gospel? The Gospel is the redeeming work of God through the life, death, burial, and the resurrection of Jesus Christ (1 Corinthians 15:3-4 NIV). It is the revelation of God's plan for reconciling man to Himself by forgiving his sin through the person and work of his Son Jesus Christ, which the church has been commissioned to proclaim. It is sometimes called the Good News of Jesus Christ.

j. What is their doctrine of Salvation? Salvation is deliverance from trouble or evil; it is the process by which God redeems His creation through the life, death, burial, and resurrection of Jesus Christ (Acts 4:12 NLT). Salvation is by the grace through faith; those who receives the Lord Jesus Christ as Savior are born again by the Holy Spirit and become the children of God.

k. What is their doctrine of The Church? The local church is a body of believers, with Christ Jesus as the Head and the Holy Spirit as its guide. The universal Church of Jesus Christ is composed solely of those who have been redeemed, regenerated, and sealed by the Holy Spirit, and that they are saved to worship and to serve. The responsibility of the Church is to win others to Jesus and to live holy lives as we honor God, by loving Him and loving others (Matthew 22:37-39; 28:19-20 KJV).

l. What is their doctrine of Marriage? The Bible teaches that marriage is ordained by God and is the union between one man and one woman. The institution of marriage is recorded in Genesis 2:23-24 (ESV). The New Testament adds a warning regarding this oneness; "So they are no longer two, but one flesh. Therefore what God has joined together, let man not separate" (Matthew 19:6 ESV).

m. What is their doctrine of Sanctity of Life? The Bible teaches that all human life is sacred and begins at conception is. The Bible never specifically addresses the issue of abortion. However, there are numerous teachings in Scripture that make it abundantly clear what God's view of abortion. Jeremiah 1:5 (NLT) tells us that God knows us before He formed us in the womb. Psalm 139:13-16 (BSB) speaks of God's active role in our creation and formation in the womb. Exodus 21:22-25 (BSB) prescribes the same penalty of someone who causes the death of a baby in the womb as the penalty for someone who commits murder. This clearly indicates that God considers a baby in the womb as just as much of a human being as a full-grown adult. For the Christian, abortion is not a matter of a woman's right to choose. It is a matter of the life or death of a human being made in God's image (Genesis 1:26-27; 9:6 KJV).

So, the first elements of a Christian Church you should look for are the church doctrinal statement and their biblical beliefs. Do they line up with the Word of God.

2. The second thing you should look for in a church is: is the Love of Christ Jesus there?

   • In John 13:34-35 (NIV), Jesus said, "A new commandment I give you: Love one another. As I have loved you, so also you must love one another. By this all men will know that you are My disciples, if you love one another."

   • Romans 12:10 (NIV), "Be devoted to one another in love. Honor one another above yourselves."

   • 1 Peter 2:17 (BSB), "Treat everyone with high regard: Love the brotherhood of believers, fear God, and honor the king."

After all that has been said about the importance of the church in the Christian life; I would like to say that the time we spend in church is a part of our Sabbath Day worship. What I mean is that when we go to church for worship, our emphasis and focus should be on the Lord Jesus Christ. The church should be the place where the body of Jesus Christ come together to worship and praise Him as is outline in chapter 9.

PRAYER:

> Lord God I pray that you would lead me to the body of saints that You would have me to be a part of. That I may serve You and others through the gifts and talents the Holy Spirit has given me. I pray that the body of believers that I fellowship with have true community. Lord Jesus please help me to remember that I bear Your name, that I am Your bride and a part of Your body . . . the Church. And, Lord I pray for spiritual growth so that I might be a blessing to the body and bring your name glory. In Jesus' name – AMEN

Reflection Time:

1. Are you a part of a Church? If not, why not? If so, what does it mean to you to be a part of the body of Christ?

    _____

    _____

    _____

    _____

    _____

    _____

2. What is NOT the Church?

    _____

    _____

    _____

    _____

    _____

    _____

3. What is the Church?

    _____

    _____

    _____

    _____

    _____

    _____

4. What are some of the reasons some people don't join the Church?

    _____

    _____

    _____

    _____

    _____

5. List some of the benefits of being a member of a Church.

    _____

    _____

    _____

_____
_____
_____

6. What is the importance of the Church?

_____
_____
_____
_____
_____
_____

7. What are some of the things you should look for in choosing a Church?

_____
_____
_____
_____
_____
_____

"Do not think that I have come to abolish the Law or the Prophets; I have not come to abolish them but to fulfill them. For truly I tell you, until heaven and earth disappear, not the smallest letter, not the least stroke of a pen, will by any means disappear from the Law until everything is accomplished. Therefore, anyone who sets aside one of the least of these commands and teaches others accordingly will be called least in the kingdom of heaven, but whoever practices and teaches these commands will be called great in the kingdom of heaven" (Matthew 5:17-19 NIV).

The Conclusion

In conclusion, I found that with pursuing holiness there are few Christians on the road to a totally surrendered life to God/Jesus. I guess Jesus meant this when He said in Matthew chapter seven: "Enter through the narrow gate. For wide is the gate and broad is the road that leads to destruction, and many enter through it. But small is the gate and narrow the road that leads to life, and only a few find it" (Matthew 7:13-14 NIV).

I'm not saying those who are totally surrendered are not saved. I'm just saying that very few believers today even understand what holiness means, or the outpouring of God that comes upon the believer that lives holy unto the Lord.

Holiness does not just happen to fall on you by accident. It requires a decision of your will, a change of mind, and an act of your faith. The individual that loves God/Jesus and keeps his commands, the Bible says that they would be loved by God the Father and Jesus the Son, and that Jesus would show himself to them (John 14:21 NIV).

Some of you may say that Jesus could live a perfect and holy life because He was God (and it is true, Jesus is God in human flesh). However, I have tried to demonstrate throughout this book that individuals such as Paul, Peter, James, John, the un-named Good Samaritan and others have demonstrated to us that ordinary people can fulfill God's commands of holiness if one desires it.

I wrote this book because I did not understand or have someone to teach me how to live as a Christian. I said the "Sinners Prayer." I asked the Lord Jesus Christ into my heart and I know that I am a born-again child of God. But I didn't know what steps to take or how to grow in the faith. I needed to know that Jesus loved me and that He wants a relationship with me. I also needed to have the biblical view of sanctification, an understanding of surrendering to God/Jesus and how to separate from this world. As a new Christian, I didn't know who I was in God/Jesus, or that He called me friend.

Learning to have a genuine Christian love for others, having the right Christian response to this evil world and having God/Jesus' biblical view about sex did not come easy. But God the Father has given us the person and the power of the Holy Spirit to help us along the way. The Holy Spirit will lead, guide, and direct our lives if we surrender every area of our lives to Him and obey His voice.

We all have the honor and privilege of praising and worshiping such a loving God because of His love, His mercy, and His grace. With worship and praise, it should come naturally to Christians, and we should also do it because He deserves it, and it's what we were created for – to praise and worship HIM throughout eternity.

After I have written these this book on pursuing holiness, I find my final conclusion also comes from the Word of God. The Old and New Testament point out to us what the key to the pursue of holiness is: "Love the Lord our God with all our hearts and with all our soul and with all our minds. Which is the first and greatest commandment, and we must also Love our neighbor as ourselves" (Matthew 22:37-40; Deuteronomy 10:12-13 NIV). Here I find the words of Solomon most appropriate: "Let us hear the conclusion of the whole matter: Fear God, and keep his commandments: for this is the whole duty of man" (Ecclesiastes 12:13 KJV).

Again, this book is a tool we can use to redirect our lives and disciple the lives of others as we fulfill the call and the command that every Christian has on their life . . . to live holy and pleasing lives unto God the Father. The Bible tells us "For God did not call us to be impure, but to live a holy life" (1 Thessalonians 4:7 NIV). "SO, PURSUE HOLINESS!"

2 Corinthians 7:1: Therefore, since we have these promises, dear friends, let us purify ourselves from everything that contaminates body and spirit, perfecting holiness out of reverence for God (NIV).

References

Chapter One: Understanding Our Sanctification

Holman Bible Publishers, "New International Version Disciple's Study Bible." (Zondervan Publishing House: Nashville, Tennessee, 1984), page 1736 Glossary of Theological Terms.

Ibid, page 1735 Glossary of Theological Terms.

Ibid, page 1738 Glossary of Theological Terms.

Chapter Two: What does Jesus want most from me?

Holman Bible Publishers, "New International Version Disciple's Study Bible." (Zondervan Publishing House: Nashville, Tennessee, 1984), page 1737 Glossary of Theological Terms.

Ingram, Chip. "Becoming A Romans 12 Coach." http:// livingontheedge.org/ and info@lote.org

Chapter Three: Totally Surrendering All

© 2007 (research from 1998 to 2006) R. J. Krejcir Ph.D., Francis A. Schaeffer Institute of Church Leadership Development. http:// www.truespirituality.org/

Ingram, Chip. "Becoming A Romans 12 Coach." http:// livingontheedge.org/ and info@lote.org.

Ibid., Book page 9.

Chapter Four: Separating from this World

Ingram, Chip. "Becoming A Romans 12 Coach." http:// livingontheedge.org/ and info@lote.org, Book page 16.

Chapter Five: Understanding Who I Really Am

Ingram, Chip. "Becoming A Romans 12 Coach." http://livingontheedge.org/ and info@lote.org.

Ibid., Book page 24.

Ingram, Chip. "Becoming A Romans 12 Coach." http://livingontheedge.org/ and info@lote.org, Book page 29.

Chapter Seven: The Christian Response to the World

Strong, James. "The New Strong's Exhaustive Concordance of the Bible." (Thomas Nelson Publishers: Nashville, Tennessee, 1984), page 15.

Ibid., page 375.

BibleStudyTool.Com. http://www.biblestudytool.com/Sexual Immorality

http://www.rayfowler.org/2008/04/18/statistics-on-living-together-before-marriage/

http://waitingtillmarriage.org/study-couples-who-waited

Reprinted from "The Real Truth About Teens and Sex" by Sabrina Weill by arrangement with Perigee Books, a member of Penguin Group USA) Inc., Copyright © 2005 by Sabrina Weill.

http://www.dosomething.org/tipsandtools/11-facts-about-teens-and-stds

http://www.teenpregnancystatistics.org/content/surviving-an-unplanned-pregnancy.html

http://www.webmd.com/sex-relationships/guide/10-surprising-health-benefits-of-sex

http://longevity.about.com/b/2007/05/23/sex-makes-you-live-longer.htm

Chapter Nine: Praise and Worship

Wikipedia – Hallelujah: en.wikipedia.org/wiki/Hallelujah

For More Information:

The Matthew 28:20 Group, LLC
P.O. Box 3613
Rock Hill, S.C. 29732

Web Site: Matthew2820group.com

Printed in the United States
by Baker & Taylor Publisher Services